D0579875

MIRACLE
ON THE
POTOMAC

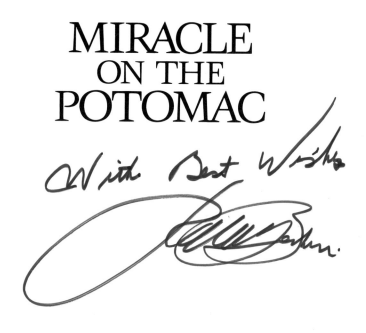

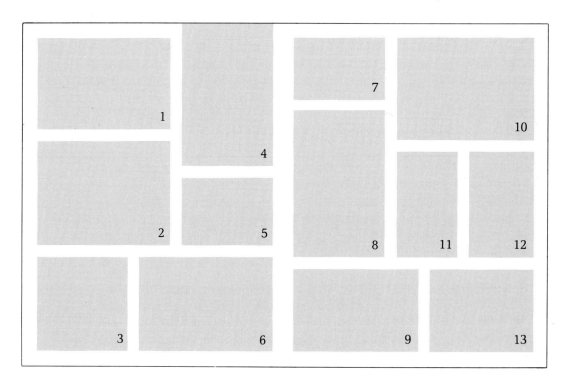

Key to endpaper photographs:

OH: Opera House   ET: Eisenhower Theater   T: Terrace Theater   TH: Theater Lab

1. *Les Miserables*, OH, December 29, 1986-February 14, 1987.
2. *Das Rheingold, Der Ring des Nibelungen*, OH, June 1-8, 1989.
3. *Shiro* (The Tokyo Kid Brothers), T, May 11-June 6, 1982.
4. Menotti's *The Consul* (Washington Opera production with Ariel Bybee and Magda Sorel), OH, May 3-10, 1975.
5. *The Country Girl* (Maureen Stapleton and Jason Robards), ET, November 16-December 14, 1971.
6. *Shear Madness*, TL, August 13, 1987-?. (Still running as of October 1989.)
7. Shanghai Acrobatic Theater, OH, April 29-May 4, 1980.
8. *The Bride from Pluto*, T, April 12-17, 1982.
9. *The Last Meeting of the Knights of the White Magnolias* (*Texas Trilogy* by Preston Jones), ET, August 5-September 12, 1976.
10. *The Time of Your Life* (Lewis J. Stadlen and Henry Fonda), ET, January 15-February 5, 1972.
11. *The Last of Mrs. Lincoln* (Julie Harris and Tobias Haller), OH, November 12-December 2, 1972.
12. Alfred Drake in *The Skin of Our Teeth*, ET, July 2-August 2, 1975.
13. *Do You Turn Somersaults?* (Anthony Quayle and Mary Martin), ET, August 17-September 24, 1977.

MIRACLE ON THE POTOMAC

The Kennedy Center from the Beginning

by
RALPH E. BECKER

Foreword by
Roger L. Stevens

A Calvin Kytle Book

Bartleby Press
Silver Spring, Maryland

Copyright © 1990 by Ralph E. Becker

All rights reserved. No part of this book may be used or reproduced in any form whatsoever without written permission except in the case of brief quotations embodies in critical reviews and articles.

Printed in the United States of America.

Library of Congress Cataloging-in-Publication Data

Becker, Ralph E., 1907—
    Miracle on the Potomac : the Kennedy Center from the beginning /
Ralph E. Becker.
       p.   cm.
    "A Calvin Kytle book."
    ISBN 0-910155-15-1 :
    1. John F. Kennedy Center for the Performing Arts (U.S.)—History.
I. Title.
NA6813.U6W33   1990
725 ' . 83 ' 09753—dc20   89—17720
                                                CIP

A Calvin Kytle Book
Published and distributed by:

Bartleby Press

11141 Georgia Avenue
Silver Spring, Maryland 20902
(301) 949-2443

To my wife, Ann,
who stood by me during my 18-year tenure as
trustee and general counsel,
and without whose dedication, persistence, and encouragement
this history would never
have been written.

A Tribute

To President Dwight D. Eisenhower, to record for posterity his major contributions to the performing arts and our cultural heritage during his terms in office, 1953 to 1960.

Portrait of President Eisenhower by J. Anthony Willis hangs in the box tier of the Eisenhower Theater.

Friend Carol Channing with founding chairman Roger L. Stevens. At the time of his appointment by President Kennedy in 1961, Stevens had been equally successful as Broadway producer, real-estate entrepreneur, and political fund-raiser. He served actively as chairman until 1988.

Foreword
by Roger L. Stevens

Although the events of the last 30 years surrounding the Kennedy Center have been written about frequently, the facts have often been distorted. Since I was involved in the establishment of the Center, as its chairman I am happy to say that Mr. Becker has done a thorough job of research and has many new and surprising facts to present to the reader. His book will be welcomed as a historical record of events that took place up to the opening night.

Ralph was himself tireless in working with me in molding the Kennedy Center into its present shape despite the many difficulties that had to be faced because of lack of funds, opposition from Capitol Hill, and the skepticism of native Washingtonians. We worked side by side in attempting to solve the various problems as they arose, and he showed great ingenuity in finding solutions.

When I first talked to President Kennedy about the National Cultural Center, as it was then known, he said he would help us in any way he could. He emphasized that he wanted the project completed as soon as possible. He felt, as I did, that for the United States, the richest nation in the world, not to have proper facilities to display its performing arts was a disgrace.

Following the tragedy of his assassination, it seemed likely that no further progress would be made and that things would come to a halt. However, such was the overwhelming respect for President Kennedy on the part of Congress and the public that the government supplied half the necessary funds toward the cost of the construction of the building, and the private sector contributed the rest. First, it was agreed that, for a memorial, more was required than just a building for the breeze to blow through. What was needed was a living memorial to a martyred American president in a place where the American performing arts could be displayed in their finest sense to the nation and to the world.

I felt I had an important mission to accomplish, but little did I know the difficulties that would have to be faced. There were strikes, shortages of money, and contractors walking off the job, to say nothing of the criticism on the Hill—all of which is set forth in detail in the body of this work.

Ralph spent a great deal of his time during the 13 years of construction and formation of the Center without anywhere near adequate compensation. I felt he should have received some reward even though he did not ask for it. He was a skillful negotiator and a driving force in getting the doors of the Kennedy Center open. Of course, many others gave generously of their time and talents toward the completion of the building and deserve great praise. In his book, Ralph has acknowledged many of these people who worked tirelessly toward that final goal. I am very mindful of the value of this help, in both funds and services, donated by so many. It is by far too long a list to incorporate in a preface, but I hope readers will understand the effort that made the building possible.

Contents

DWIGHT EISENHOWER:
Advocate in Chief for the Performing Arts

*I*n October 1800, when John Adams arrived to take up residence in the White House, the city of Washington was hardly a sight to lift the spirits. Except for what was then called the Presidential Palace and the square Senate wing of the Capitol still under construction, the only buildings were a few boardinghouses—so few that the 32 senators and 106 representatives who came for the first congressional session in the new capital had no choice other than to share beds or sleep on the floors. In the words of one congressman, the outdoor scene was "melancholy and ludicrous." Wherever one turned, the virtually unrelieved view was of tree stumps (acres of them), cornstalks, marshlands, excavation holes, and litter.

And yet less than a month later, on November 20, our second president looked out on this ugly, messy landscape and gave his countrymen a vision that in time would become a mandate. Here on the wooded banks of the Potomac, John Adams saw "the capital of a great nation advancing with unexampled rapidity in arts, in commerce, in wealth, and in population."

It was not until 1971, with the opening of the John F. Kennedy Center for the Performing Arts, that the nation's capital began to advance in the arts with the rapidity that Adams prophesied. In *Miracle on the Potomac*, I have sought to show how this came about, to recount the Center's long, often controversial, and heretofore untold history. But I have had another purpose in writing this book: to pay tribute to President Dwight D. Eisenhower for something most of us tend to forget. It was Eisenhower who, on September 2, 1958, signed the legislation authorizing

President Eisenhower saw the performing arts as an integral part of his program to promote better understanding among peoples of the world, a program that included a larger budget for the Voice of America, higher status for the U.S. Information Agency, and the introduction of People-to-People.

a national cultural center. What is now the Kennedy Center began under his administration.

To be reminded of President Eisenhower's seminal contribution in no way diminishes the appropriateness of the Center as a living memorial to John F. Kennedy. President Kennedy's love for the arts and the importance he gave them in the achievement of national goals are as much a part of the Center as its architecture, and they always will be. But to neglect the role that Eisenhower played in the Center's chancy beginnings not only omits a significant item of cultural history but also serves to perpetuate an image of the man that does disservice to his memory.

During his lifetime and since his death, most historians have focused with good reason on Eisenhower's accomplishments as soldier and statesman. But there was more to Eisenhower, even the *public* Eisenhower, than his effectiveness as a leader in difficult times. One man who knew this other side very well is his former speech writer William Bragg Ewald, Jr., who, when asked to describe the Eisenhower he knew, usually defers to the poet Carl Sandburg: "steel and velvet . . . as hard as rock and soft as drifting fog." To Ewald, as he was to Sandburg, Eisenhower was "one who held in his heart and mind the paradox of terrible storm and peace unspeakable and perfect."

It is undoubtedly from these commonly overlooked qualities—the "velvet" and the "heart" in him—that Eisenhower's commitment to the arts derived. For him, the arts were part of a much larger quest for better understanding among the peoples of the world. Programs like People-to-People, which encouraged Americans of all races, creeds, and occupations to visit and communicate with their counterparts in many different lands, had his enthusiastic endorsement. Artists were routinely included in such programs, and they got more focused support through the cultural exchange agreements initiated by his State Department. Further evidence of his interest came through the changing nature of cultural performances at the White House, which during his years there moved from entertainment by military ensembles and pop stars to concerts by renowned artists of opera, ballet, and symphony. It was an interest, moreover, that did not stop at the White House gates.

The president demonstrated his personal interest in the performing arts by participating in the ground-breaking ceremony for the Lincoln Center in New York on May 14, 1959.

My role in the building of the national cultural center began officially in 1959, when President Eisenhower appointed me founding trustee and general counsel. President Richard Nixon reappointed me, and I served until 1976, when President Gerald Ford sent me to Honduras as U.S. ambassador (1976-77). Congress awarded me the title of Honorary Trustee in 1980. I was thus very much involved in the Center's birth and maturation. It has been an exhilarating experience, some measure of which I hope to convey in the story that follows. It has provided me with a wonderful opportunity to work with dedicated people in both public and private sectors, people who have given time and money to a project that has enhanced the life of both the capital and the country. Many of these I mention in the narrative; those with whom I had less contact are listed in the acknowledgments.

NOT SURPRISINGLY, serving as counsel to the Center had the effect of stimulating my interest in history. What I soon discovered—hardly an original observation—was that Washington's cultural life has always been intimately connected to the official Washington, to the Washington of ceremony and monuments. Military music, of course, has been a fixture of state occasions from the beginning days of the Republic. Military bands began with "the President's own"—the U.S. Marine Band—which, when President Adams established it in 1798, consisted of "a drum major, fife major and 32 drums and fifes." Subsequently, other military branches formed musical groups, although it was not until 1922 that an official Army band was designated and not until 1923 that the Navy followed suit. The Air Force band achieved official status in 1941.

The first known theatrical performance in the capital occurred in 1800, four months before John Adams moved into the White House. It was held in a bare room in a still unfinished hotel that one patron described as "astonishingly dirty and void of decoration," where the audience sat uncomfortably "amidst tobacco smoke, whiskey breaths, and other stenches, mixed up with the effluvia of stables and miasma of the canal." Staged by a touring Philadelphia company, the drama was forced to close after one of the shortest runs on record; all the props and costumes were destroyed by a flood on the Mall caused by an overflow from Tiber Creek.

The capital got its first theater four years later. It was called, appropriately, the Washington Theater, and this time the ambience of opening night was worth a good review. "The house is fitted up with great neatness," read an account in the *National Intelligencer.* "The whole house, the stage as well as that part occupied by the audience, appears like one elegant room, happily proportioned and neatly furnished."

Since that opening, the capital has had no fewer than 150 theaters of one sort or another offering live entertainment. Most of these are now gone, razed for other, newer buildings constructed for other purposes. This was the fate, for example, of the 2,000-seat Albaugh's Opera House, re-named Poli's, which was torn down in the early 1930s as part of the Federal Triangle project. The Shubert-Belasco, built in 1907 as the Lafayette Square Opera House, occupied a prime location, catty-corner to the White House on the east side of Lafayette Square. After serving as the Stage Door Canteen during World War II, it was demolished to make way for the present Court of Claims building, a cornerstone of the National Place Reconstruction. Some facilities did not even last until the twentieth century. Willard Hall, a site now occupied by the west addition to the historic Willard Hotel, was not restored after a fire in 1866.

The National Theatre, fifth building on its site on E Street, now Pennsylvania Avenue, dates from 1835. Fires, so prevalent in nineteenth-century theaters, and even the total reconstruction of the block between E and F streets, mattered not to the ghosts of this most historic spot of Washington theater lore. It was here that her mother took five-year-old Helen Hayes to see her first play. She would first perform publicly as a child at the Lafayette Square Opera House and the Columbia Theatre (also now vanished) but would return to the National many times during her long reign as First Lady of the American Theater. The mezzanine lounge, now boasting a small stage for nonprofit performances, is named in her honor. Practically every president since Andrew Jackson has attended performances at the National, and over the years its stage has been hospitable to every known form of drama, from *Ben Hur* (which featured 350 actors and eight horses) to *Cats.*

Of more recent origins than the National but with almost as many incarnations is the Lincoln Theatre, built in 1912 to serve Washington's black community. Unique in that it housed both an auditorium and a ballroom, the Lincoln is remembered for its lavish plaster decorations, eight round boxes, gilded ceiling, and soft red velvet seats. It was billed as "Washington's Black Broadway," over the years presenting stars such as Duke Ellington, Bessie Smith, and Louis Armstrong, and attracting patrons from the District, Maryland, and Virginia. Sadly, after the riots of 1968 it fell rapidly into disrepair, and when it closed in 1983 it was showing mostly horror movies. In 1989 the Lincoln was being spiritedly restored by a group of private citizens with the help of a $4 million government grant. Under the leadership of Francine Cohen and the Lincoln Theatre Foundation, it is due to reopen in 1991, coincidental with the completion of a subway stop across the street, as a showcase for the performing arts. Once again it promises to be "the jewel of U Street."

Before the Kennedy Center was completed, perhaps the most important auditorium in Washington was Constitution Hall, dedicated by the Daughters of the American Revolution on April 29, 1929. Constitution Hall seats 4,000, and though built for the DAR's national conventions, it is leased out on many occasions for concerts and served for many years as the home of the National Symphony. Two other important facilities are Lisner Auditorium at the George Washington University and the Coolidge Auditorium at the Library of Congress, though gone is the vast, acoustically poor Washington Auditorium on the site of the Interior Department.

It cannot be said, then, that Washington was without venues for theater and music when President Eisenhower took office in 1953. What *can* be said, without question, is that no facility in Washington compared with the best in other capitals of the world. Especially lacking were theaters designed for ballet and grand opera. At home in Moscow, for instance, the Bolshoi Ballet was accustomed to a stage 200 feet in depth; by contrast, the stage of the old Loew's Capitol, where the company appeared in 1962, measured a bare 26 feet. Paul Hume, emeritus music editor for the *Washington Post*, recalls vividly what visiting artists used to face:

> On its first visit to the United States back in 1949, the Royal Ballet, having danced superbly in the old Metropolitan Opera House in New York, came to Washington—where, alas, the best and largest place appeared to be Constitution Hall. I was, therefore, among the thousands who saw Margot Fonteyn, then one of the world's most

radiantly beautiful ballerinas, make her entrance as Odette in *Swan Lake*, take three or four steps on the stage, and, slipping, fall flat on her exquisite *derriere*. The floor had been *waxed*!

Nor was I the only person to hear Sir Rudolph Bing, as general director of the Metropolitan Opera, say, with an oath, after his company had played *Tosca* in the old Capitol Theater, "I will never bring this company to this city again until there is a decent place in which I can appear." That night it had taken longer to change the scenery between acts one and two than it took to perform the entire second act.

By the early 1950s, many people had come to think that Washington's cultural life did not befit the great power that the United States had become. The cold war was making the country much more self-conscious. There was increasing recognition of the need generally to articulate our ideals and standards to the rest of the world, and particularly to add a dimension to the image of Washington that would convey the country's aesthetic as well as its political values. Then, too, with its growth during and after World War II, the city had drawn to its swelling population the kind of educated professionals for whom the theater and the arts were integral parts of a lifestyle.

Eisenhower, the professional military man, had observed firsthand the impact of propaganda during World War II, and from this experience he had learned something about psychological warfare. Equally significant, despite the institutionalized inhumanity of the Nazis and the impartial carnage of combat, what Eisenhower saw of men and women in wartime only served to reinforce his basic faith in the good will and good sense of ordinary people. "People want peace so badly," he once observed, "that someday governments are going to have to get out of the way and let them have it."

It was only logical, therefore, that one of his first acts as president was to create a commission to study means of better fighting the psychological battles of the cold war. One consequence was an expanded broadcast operation—under a substantially larger budget—of the Voice of America. Another was the issuance of an executive order creating the United States Information Agency, the effect of which was to consolidate all overseas information activities of the State Department into a separate bureau reporting directly to the White House. He appointed a former head of the Mutual Broadcasting System, Theodore Streibert, as the first USIA director, and, as if to leave no question of the importance propaganda would have in the conduct of his foreign policy, he made Streibert a member of the National Security Council.* That he meant the USIA to be far more than political dressing was additionally evidenced by his appointment of a White House staffer to be Streibert's deputy. That staffer was an extraordinarily able administrator named Abbott Washburn, who had been an aide to presidential assistant C. D. Jackson. Washburn served under two succeeding USIA directors and into a few months of the Kennedy administration, providing continuity and stability to an executive function for which there was no peacetime precedent.

In September 1956, Eisenhower convened a two-day meeting of a hundred distinguished Americans to consider new ways for increasing contacts among ordinary citizens and their counterparts in other countries. The group included not only business, labor, military, and academic leaders, but also artists such as conductor Eugene Ormandy and novelist William Faulkner. Out of this conference came the People-to-People program, which made real something the president had been thinking about since before taking office. Speaking to the conferees, Eisenhower outlined his objective. It was "for people to get together and to leap governments—if necessary to evade governments—to work out not one method but thousands of methods by which people can gradually learn a bit more of each other. . . . This way, I believe, is the truest path to peace." The president clearly had in mind people from behind the iron curtain as well as those from America's allies and the developing world. After meeting Nikita Khrushchev in Geneva in 1955, he had said, "What we must do is consider every possible chink in the iron curtain. And bring the people behind that curtain into our curtain." The spirit of the program has endured to the present, as evidenced by President Ronald Reagan's reference to it during Mikhail Gorbachev's visit to the United States in December 1987.

People-to-People was organized as a national citizens' program, with

---

* With an obviously different view of propaganda's place in security strategies, McGeorge Bundy, national security adviser to President Kennedy, removed the USIA director from the NSC.

Prominent in the group that met with President Eisenhower to launch his People-to-People program in September 1956 were spokespersons for the arts such as Mrs. Jouett Shouse, philanthropist and one of the founding trustees of the Kennedy Center; Chairman David Finley of the Commission of Fine Arts; and Eric Johnson, president of the Motion Picture Association.

people all over the country taking the initiative. While the program could count on the support of the White House and the USIA, it was a grass-roots activity, not something run by bureaucrats in Washington. Out of it have come countless projects for improving understanding between Americans and people all over the world. Trips and meetings have been arranged for all kinds of individuals to learn more about one another. Cities here and abroad have adopted each other as "sister cities." Local People-to-People programs, like the one in Minneapolis, have worked on behalf of handicapped children in Morocco and Chile and supported the efforts of the Abandoned Boys Society in Sierra Leone. Foreign and American scholars, lawyers, doctors, and artists have traveled to all parts of the world for discussions and performances.

People-to-People's music committee made a major contribution to the performing arts in postwar America. The committee, chaired by people of the caliber of Eugene Ormandy and Mrs. Jouett Shouse, encouraged American artists to enter foreign musical competitions. Such events made the careers of many major artists, among them Van Cliburn, who in 1958 won the International Tchaikovsky Competition in Moscow. His achievement, and that of many another talented American in international competition, also served to soften the image of America abroad.*

That the arts transcended language and could promote "world friendship" was something Eisenhower understood well. Concerned that too many foreign peoples saw us as materialistic and militaristic, he felt strongly that performances of our artists could make an implicit statement to the contrary. It was a point he made vigorously in his 1954 message to Congress requesting $5 million for cultural exchange programs. Thus, it was not by happenstance that these first funds were used to send the New York Philharmonic on a Latin American tour, and the Philadelphia and Boston symphony orchestras, the New York City Ballet, and major individual artists to the capitals of Europe. These same funds sent an American company of the Gershwin opera, *Porgy and Bess*, to Europe and, through Soviet financing, to Moscow, a cultural exchange that was not entirely faithfully recorded by Truman Capote in his book *The Muses Are Heard*.

Eisenhower discussed the need for a government commission on the arts as early as January 1955. At that time he apparently envisaged for Washington a dedicated public building, whose architecture would symbolize the nation's desire for international understanding and whose concert halls would provide foreign tourists with a steady display of America's aesthetic sensibilities, a side they rarely had a chance to see. While cultivating this idea, in January 1958 he achieved a significant breakthrough with a far-reaching exchange agreement with the Soviet Union, through which both countries were opened up to each other's scholars, artists, and scientists. As part of this arrangement, the Bolshoi Opera came here and the New York Philharmonic traveled there.

To a modest degree, the Eisenhowers used the White House as a showcase for this same purpose. There is a touch of irony here. Eisenhower's predecessor, Harry Truman, played the piano with the skill of a gifted amateur and had a lifelong affection for the classics. Yet formal

* For this account of the arts during the Eisenhower years, I have found Elise K. Kirk, *Music at the White House: A History of the American Spirit* (Urbana and Chicago: University of Illinois Press, 1986), 266-277, to be most helpful.

PROGRAM

HIRAM SHERMAN

Steam Heat	PAT STANLEY
"Pajama Game"	FRANK DERBAS
	PETER GENNARO

Balcony Scene	CAROL LAWRENCE
Tonight	LARRY KERT
"West Side Story"	

Trouble	EDDIE HODGES
Gary, Indiana	
"Music Man"	

You're My Friend, Ain'tcha?	
"New Girl in Town"	THELMA RITTER
	CAMERON PRUD'HOMME

I Could Have Danced All Night	
Show Me	
"My Fair Lady"	SALLY ANN HOWES

At Eisenhower's invitation, artists appeared regularly at White House dinners for foreign dignitaries. What in subsequent administrations became nationally televised events ("In Performance at the White House") began with this 1958 program featuring stars from popular musicals then running on Broadway.

musical programs were held at the White House during only one of the eight years of the Truman presidency. It remained for Eisenhower, whose own tastes ran to the popular and sentimental (he liked Lawrence Welk and once listed his favorite song as "One Dozen Roses"), to make musicales—24 of them in all—a regular feature of state dinners. The artists brought to the Executive Mansion for such occasions represented a fair cross-section of American music, with one notable exception: the East Room was off limits to bop, rock 'n' roll, and electronic jazz. The Army's Singing Sergeants and the Air Force's Strolling Strings performed with the frequency of resident companies. Fred Waring and his chorus of Pennsylvanians performed three times, once for visiting Queen Elizabeth II and Prince Philip of England. Other evenings were brightened by appearances of artists as varied as the Deep River Boys, the Mormon Tabernacle Choir, Arthur Rubinstein, the Trapp Family Singers, Leon Fleischer, and Gregor Piatigorsky. During one memorable evening, with Leonard Bernstein as soloist, 44 members of the New York Philharmonic performed two concertos.

Talent abounded in a White House program I helped put together on

May 8, 1958, with Harold Prince and his partner, Robert Griffith, both protégés of George Abbott. (Prince and Abbott have since been named Kennedy Center honorees.) Following a dinner for Chief Justice Earl Warren, guests were treated to a "first," an evening devoted to the music of five Broadway musicals.* We brought nine stars from these shows to perform for the president and his 150 guests. It was a great evening, although some New York critics scolded us for taking the stars away from their scheduled performances.

During these years artists got the presidential stamp in several other conspicuous ways, a noteworthy example being Eisenhower's presentation in 1955 of a congressional gold medal to songwriter Irving Berlin. All these activities drew attention to the arts as important to the life of the United States, and they undoubtedly enhanced the president's eagerness to develop a national cultural center. The arts, he believed, should not be an elitist activity, and the White House should not be their only government-endorsed showcase in Washington.

An example of this commitment was Eisenhower's support of efforts to restore Ford's Theatre, the historic site of Abraham Lincoln's assassination. In the 1950s, with the approach of the Civil War centennial, this effort was getting renewed attention. Prominent figures in Congress favored the restoration, as did influential local residents and institutions such as the Library of Congress's Lincoln scholar, David Mearns; the chairman of Catholic University's drama department, Rev. Gilbert V. Hartke; the Lincoln Group, including historian and representative Fred Schwengel (R-Iowa); and the Cultural Development Committee of the Board of Trade. The effort was bipartisan, led by Republican senator Milton Young of North Dakota and Democratic National Committee member Melvin Hildreth of the District of Columbia. I worked especially closely with Senator Young, Rep. Michael J. Kirwan (D-Ohio), Sherman Adams, and Cornelius W. Heine of the National Park Service (NPS).

Eisenhower was the first president to sign a bill authorizing the restoration, and in 1956 planning was advanced with introduction of his

---

* The nine stars who left their Broadway engagements to sing for the president and his guests were Pat Stanley, Frank Derbas, and Peter Gennaro of *Pajama Game*; Carol Lawrence and Larry Kert of *West Side Story*; Eddie Hodges of *Music Man*; Thelma Ritter and Cameron Prud'homme of *New Girl in Town*; and Sally Ann Howes of *My Fair Lady*.

Eisenhower was the first president to promote legislation for the restoration of Ford's Theatre.

Mission 66 Program. This 10-year effort of the NPS included Ford's, Independence Hall, and the Blue Ridge Parkway among an ambitious number of projects designed to preserve and enrich the nation's history. Congress provided the necessary funding in 1960. Sadly, by the time the revitalized theater opened eight years later, most people had forgotten the decisive role that Eisenhower had played.

2

GENESIS:
The National Cultural Center Act of 1958

From the thirties on, beginning perhaps with the launching of the WPA Theater under Franklin Roosevelt's New Deal, the idea for some sort of congressionally chartered auditorium surfaced periodically in Washington. All these proposals were short-lived, however, for none was ever considered politically expedient. In a town where serious men were expected to be preoccupied with problems of justice, economic depression, and the prospects of war, it seemed more than a bit frivolous to think of spending tax dollars in the support of popular entertainment or, worse, in the encouragement of something as intangible and as uncertain of payoff as "the arts." Until the end of World War II and the inauguration of President Eisenhower, *culture* was a prissy word in most Washington circles and a dirty word in many.

During the fifties, however, America came into unprecedented prosperity and the climate began to change. All across the country, arts groups experienced a surging increase in patronage, both public and private. For the first time, museums, libraries, and municipal theaters enjoyed a status on the planning agenda of city councils and chambers of commerce commonly accorded convention halls. As a consequence, enough arts centers went up in rapidly urbanizing America to give a focus to musical performance and dance that neither had ever known before. It was a trend greatly accelerated by the coming of television and the invention of the long-playing microgroove recording, and it was merely a matter of time before it reached the banks of the Potomac.

In 1948 Pennsylvania Republicans sent to Congress a former concert artist, schoolteacher, and band conductor named Carroll Kearns. Kearns had a B.M. degree from the Chicago College of Music, which he had earned during off-hours from a job on the railroad. Although he played the piano and violin professionally, he was best known as a baritone soloist, and for several seasons he had toured with Mary Garden. Once in Congress he busied himself commendably with all kinds of legislation in the interest of public education, but closest to his music-loving heart was the dream of an opera house in Washington. Toward this end, he introduced in the House essentially the same bill, session after session.

Nothing happened, however, until 1953. That year Kearns teamed up with a New Jersey Democrat, Charles D. Howell, and the pair introduced legislation to establish a commission for a national war memorial theater and opera house, to be financed with federal funds. A companion Senate bill attracted as sponsors Hubert Humphrey (D-Minn.), Estes Kefauver (D-Tenn.), and William Langer (R-N.D.). This time the Kearns bill actually got a hearing, at which these and other prominent congressmen from both parties testified in favor. The bill died, however, with adjournment of the 83d Congress.

Charles Howell did not run for reelection, but at the beginning of the 84th Congress, Kearns recruited Howell's successor, Frank Thompson, Jr. (D-N.J.), and under their cosponsorship the bill was revived. It had the conspicuous support of Eisenhower's efficient chief of staff, Sherman Adams, a man known for his love of the theater. Hearings were held on February 15 and 23, 1955, before a special subcommittee for the District of Columbia chaired by Rep. James H. Morrison (D-La.), from which emerged House Resolution (H.R.) 1825. This became the basis for Public Law (P.L.) 128 creating the D.C. Auditorium Commission. President Eisenhower signed it on July 1.

The act established a 21-member bipartisan commission to formulate "plans for the design, location, financing and construction in the District of Columbia for a civic auditorium including an Inaugural Hall of Presidents and a music, fine arts and mass communications center." On September 19, 1955, President Eisenhower appointed seven members.

Seven each were also appointed by Vice President Richard Nixon and Speaker of the House Samuel Rayburn of Texas.*

Under the legislation, the commission was due to report its recommendations before February 1, 1956. The appointments had been made so late, however, that members found it impossible to meet that deadline, a matter Congress remedied by passing P.L. 491. Signed by the president on April 27, 1956, it extended the deadline to January 31, 1957, and authorized appropriations (later specified to be $150,000) "to carry out the purposes of this Act." Interestingly, it is in the language of this act that for the first time one finds reference to a *national* cultural center.

On January 31, 1957, right on time, the commission issued a 95-page report with plans for a $36 million "National Civic Auditorium and Cultural Center for Citizens of the United States." Included in the proposal were "a great hall" with movable chairs for 10,000; a 100,000-square-foot auditorium/music hall (seating capacity 3,800-4,200) to be used for dance and theater performances and concerts; a theater to seat 1,400-1,800; a tourist information center and mass communications facility; exhibit areas; meeting rooms; and a restaurant. The commission also recommended parking accommodations for 1,500-2,000 cars. And finally, it recommended that the auditorium be located in an area known as Foggy Bottom South, which at the time consisted of 26.9 gross acres, an area that ultimately would include the Kennedy Center, the Watergate Complex, and the embassy of Saudi Arabia.

On February 6, several weeks after his second inauguration, President Eisenhower met with commission members, giving their proposal his wholehearted support. Over the next two days, the Senate-House Subcommittee of the District of Columbia met to consider it. Agnes Meyer, commission chairman, conveyed the president's endorsement and underscored the arguments for the Foggy Bottom location, citing recommendations of the seven architectural firms that together served as con-

* President Eisenhower's appointees were Mrs. Robert Low Bacon, Robert V. Fleming, Elizabeth Butler Howry, Frank R. Jellef, James L. Knight, George L. Murphy, and George Williams. Vice President Nixon's appointees were Sens. Matthew M. Neely (D-W.Va.), J. Glenn Beall (R-Md.), and Patrick McNamara (D-Mich.), and citizens Dr. George Johnson, Agnes E. Meyer, Barney Balaban, and Libby Rowe. Speaker of the House Rayburn named Reps. Carroll O. Kearns, James H. Morrison, Frank Thompson, Jr., Arthur G. Klein (D-N.Y.), and Joel T. Broyhill (R-Va.), and citizens Robert W. Dowling and Barney Breeskin.

sultants to the commission. During the hearing, companion bills were introduced into the House (H.R. 3337) and the Senate (S. 685) to prolong the life of the commission until the center could be completed.

The subcommittee to which the Senate bill was referred approved a measure directing the D.C. Auditorium Commission to select one specific site. The subcommittee, headed by Wayne Morse (D-Ore.), also recommended changing the name of the commission to the Commission for a National Cultural Center. With such a favorable atmosphere in Congress, the members moved quickly. One week later, on February 15, 1957, they voted unanimously for the Foggy Bottom site. On April 18 a Senate-House conference gave its approval, and on May 15 the Senate approved the Senate-House conference report, authorizing the General Services Administration (GSA) to acquire the tract.

By this time, however, significant opposition had surfaced to Congress's choice of the Foggy Bottom site, and opponents were prompted to take a public stand. Setting off the fireworks was Republican freshman congressman Joel Broyhill of Virginia, one of Speaker Rayburn's appointees to the commission, who favored a site in Southwest Washington then under redevelopment. He was joined by powerful local forces—George A. Garrett, president of the 25-member Federal City Council; John Remon, chairman of the Redevelopment Land Agency; Harland Bartholomew, head of the National Capital Planning Commission (NCPC); and the Greater Washington Board of Trade,* the oldest and largest business, real estate, banking, and professional organization in the city. From outside the city came dissent from William Zeckendorf of Webb and Knapp, a firm developing an area in Southwest Washington now known as L'Enfant Plaza. He wanted the center as a part of his project. Other formidable opponents were Royce F. Ward of the large Potomac Plaza Apartment and Office Building Complex, who feared the Foggy Bottom site would require moving the important Inner Loop Freeway,** which would, in turn, damage his project; and Peoples Life Insurance Company, which feared dis-

---

* When I joined the Board of Trade, it was called the Washington Board of Trade. In 1959 the name was changed to the Metropolitan Board of Trade, and in 1979 it was again changed to the Greater Washington Board of Trade.

** What was then called the Inner Loop Freeway is now the "spaghetti" of approaches to Interstates 50, 66, and 95, and to E Street, Virginia Avenue, and the Whitehurst Freeway.

ruption of its own plans to construct buildings in the Foggy Bottom area.

Controversy over the Foggy Bottom site all but ended the project, the death blow apparently dealt by Broyhill, aided and abetted by Reps. Dewitt S. Hyde (R-Md.) and Joseph P. O'Hara (D-Minn.). Under mounting pressure, on August 8, 1957, the House Appropriations Committee refused the Auditorium Commission both a $25,000 operation budget and a requested extension of time.

Though disappointed, Meyer did not despair. She knew there was important support for the cultural center, notably from the president of the American Institute of Architects and former head of the Greater Washington Board of Trade, Leon Chatelain, Jr. In Congress, she could list among the project's champions Senators Morse, Neely, McNamara, and Beall and Representatives Morrison, Kearns, Howell, Klein, Kirwan, and John L. McMillan (D-S.C.). Not to be discounted was the continuous encouragement of President Eisenhower and his chief of staff, Sherman Adams.

Perseverance paid off. Like the phoenix rising from its own ashes, the cultural center was able to regenerate itself. On January 8, 1958, Representative Thompson introduced H.R. 9848 (in a later mutation, H.R. 13017), and on February 24 Sen. J. William Fulbright (D-Ark.) introduced a companion bill, S. 3335. There then ensued a protracted battle for a site.

Both bills would have placed the center on what became known, in the heated debate they precipitated, as the Mall site. Each directed the Smithsonian Institution and its board of regents to

> provide for a National Capital Center of the Performing Arts, which will be constructed with funds raised by voluntary contributions, on part of the land in the District of Columbia made available for the Smithsonian Gallery of Art.

The bills additionally provided that the Smithsonian

> utilize so much of that tract of land in the District of Columbia referred to in the first section of the Resolution of May 17, 1938 (20 USC 76) as is bounded by Fourth Street, S.W. on the east; Seventh Street, S.W. on the west; Independence Avenue on the south; and Adams Drive on the north, title to which is in the United States. [It shall] include an auditorium, which shall be known as the Hall of

Statesmen where great statesmen, particularly Presidents and Vice Presidents, Members of the Congress including Speaker of the House of Representatives Rayburn and former Speaker [Joseph] Martin and distinguished officials of the executive and judicial branches of the Government of the United States who have contributed to an increased national recognition of the interrelation of the arts and sciences and their basic importance to a true and balanced development of American life, shall be honored and memorialized in an appropriate manner.

The Regents shall make provision for parking facilities in the vicinity of the National Capital Center of the Performing Arts and for landscaping the grounds surrounding the [center].

But by stipulating a site on the Mall, both bills were in conflict with S. 1985, which authorized plans and specifications for the construction of a national air museum almost on the same site. That bill had been introduced by Sen. Clinton P. Anderson (D-N.M.), a member of the board of regents of the Smithsonian, on July 2, 1957. A companion bill (H.R. 8513) was introduced in the House by Democratic congressman Olin E. "Tiger" Teague of Texas. Indeed, the idea for an air museum on the Mall went back to studies done in the 1930s. The museum itself was authorized in May 1936, and in 1938 a presidential advisory board had recommended its construction on the Mall.

In effect, Thompson and Fulbright attempted to preempt the site designated for the air museum. But by the time their legislation was in the hopper, the museum practically had a lock on the Mall. At least six months before the introduction of the center bills, recommendations to locate the museum there had been approved by the Air Force (on behalf of the Defense Department), GSA, the Smithsonian's board of regents, and the Commission of Fine Arts.

The executive agencies registered their resistance to the Thompson-Fulbright site proposal with mounting vehemence throughout the spring and summer of 1958. On April 17, 1958, only a few days before hearings were scheduled before the Senate Public Works Committee, GSA once again let it be known that it agreed with the Air Force. That same day, the Bureau of the Budget dispatched a letter to committee Chairman

Dennis Chavez (D-N.M.) that reiterated the administration's support for a national cultural center but, demurring from the clause in S. 3335 that would locate the center on the Mall, reminded the committee "that a number of agencies, including the bureau, have already endorsed the proposed site . . . as a location for the National Air Museum." Next day, the Commission of Fine Arts said essentially the same thing. In a statement endorsing the Anderson bill to create the air museum, Senator McNamara referred pointedly to the conflict with S. 3335: "boundary lines on three sides of a parcel of ground are mentioned in both bills." Resolution of the conflict was left to Senator Chavez and his Public Works Committee.

The outpouring of support for the air museum should not suggest that the location of the cultural center on the Mall was without advocates. There were many prominent citizens of Washington and representatives of national organizations who vigorously promoted a national cultural center on the Mall.*

At the time this debate was taking place, I was serving as chairman of the Cultural Development Committee of the Board of Trade (1954-59). In that position I sought to bring the business community together with Washington's cultural community, concentrating on what I perceived to be their mutual interest in the creation of a performing arts center. Involved as I had been in the Eisenhower campaigns of 1952 and 1956, I had come to know a number of figures prominent in the administration, among them Sherman Adams. Talks with them soon convinced me that in both the public and private sectors there were more than enough proponents of the air museum to get it built on the Mall. I did not want to see the cultural center lost because it could not be placed there as well.

Also at the time, the Board of Trade had as its executive vice president a native Washingtonian and a former officer in the Corps of Engineers named William Press. Press was on first-name terms with the city's power structure, he knew Capitol Hill intimately, and he could weave his way through the federal bureaucracy with the sure-footedness of a ballet dancer. Besides these gifts, as an engineer he knew a lot more than the rest of us about the requirements of public buildings—the critical relationship, for instance, of site to function, which was something I was beginning to

* The most prominent of these are listed on page 202.

20

think the center's most vocal advocates might be overlooking. Concerned by what appeared to be a developing stalemate, I met with him on several occasions to explore suitable alternative locations. One day, he came to me with a fateful suggestion. "Ralph," he said, "General Welling wants us to meet him at the Lincoln Memorial. I think he may have an answer for us."

Gen. Alvin Welling represented the Corps of Engineers on the District's three-man Board of Commissioners, which Congress had designated to administer the city when the commission form of government was established in the 1870s. Several years before our introduction, he had been authorized by Congress to plan a bridge across the Potomac to link up with a new complex of roads (the so-called Inner Loop Freeway) and Virginia. The corps had proposed a bridge that would require footings on Theodore Roosevelt Island, but its proposal had run into sharp opposition from conservationists and the Fine Arts Commission. His opponents, General Welling observed, plainly did not want "to touch one blade of grass on the bird sanctuary," and he was having quite a problem trying to locate the bridge elsewhere.

To orient us, General Welling unrolled a sheaf of drawings and spread them out on the marble floor of the Lincoln Memorial. He directed our eyes first to a spot on a map, then to a site on Constitution Avenue near 24th Street, then to a large open area adjacent. "Help me get my bridge located," he said and paused, pointing successively to several places on the map, "—here, here, or here, I don't give a damn where, but it's got to be located—and we'll give you this Foggy Bottom area for a cultural center."

What the general offered us was a magnificent site, a piece of the same Foggy Bottom South that the D.C. Auditorium Commission had preferred but failed to get. It was larger than the inconvenient Mall site and in every way superior. Press and I responded with like excitement and like minds. I promised Welling that I would do everything I could to obtain the administration's support for a location for the bridge acceptable to the corps, and everything in my power to win acceptance of the Potomac River site in Foggy Bottom as the one most suitable for the cultural center.

Shortly thereafter I met with Frederick Seaton, secretary of Interior, and then I visited Sherman Adams, who had already proven himself an invaluable ally. In short order, Seaton and Adams gave the administration's blessing to a location for what is now the Theodore Roosevelt

Bridge.* Almost at the same time, the deal was consummated with General Welling for the Potomac River site for the cultural center.

THE TIMING OF THIS ARRANGEMENT was fortunate because I was now due to testify at hearings of the Senate Public Works Committee. As I read the political situation, the air museum had clearly won the battle for the Mall site. So, with Press's support and that of the president and directors of the Board of Trade, I intended to propose the Potomac River setting as an alternative—and preferred—site for the center. In moving forward I knew I had the support of Sherman Adams, who spoke for President Eisenhower. Equally important, I knew I could count on certain influential members of Congress—in particular, the chairman of the committee, the powerful senator from New Mexico, Dennis Chavez. I had been told by Senator Chavez's son, who had worked for me in my law office, that his father would surely support my position since his New Mexico colleague, Clinton Anderson, was quarterback for the air museum on the Mall site and Chavez was pledged to vote with him. Subsequently, my proposal won the blessing of the ranking Republican on the committee, John Sherman Cooper of Kentucky. Later, he and Chavez's successor on the committee, Senator McNamara, would prove invaluable in pushing the project along, as would their colleagues on the committee, Sens. Roman Hruska (R-Neb.), Norris Cotton (R-N.H.), and Edward Martin (R-Pa.).

I appeared at a hearing of the committee on April 22 and 23, 1958, testifying on behalf of the Board of Trade. In my testimony I first cited the advantages of the 13-acre Potomac River site—its accessibility; its aesthetic virtues; its proximity to public transportation, hotels, restaurants, and parking facilities. I then went on to point out the risks involved if the center's proponents sought to take from the Smithsonian the Mall site designated for the air museum. To advocate the same site for both projects, I said, would lead to a prolonged stalemate resulting in the completion of neither project.

I was the only person testifying for the Potomac River site, and I was especially apprehensive about the reaction of Senator Fulbright, who was a

* This satisfactorily resolved the problem of placement of supports. The law authorizing construction of the bridge was signed by President Eisenhower on June 4, 1958.

fervent advocate of the Mall site. Anticipating his displeasure, I phoned Mrs. Robert Low Bacon* at her home in Alexandria Bay, N.Y., asking her to send a statement to her good friend Senator Fulbright for insertion in the *Congressional Record*. She agreed, and shortly thereafter the senator read her comments into the *Record*, but if they had any moderating effect on Fulbright I'll never know. Just as I feared, he cross-examined me sharply about both the Potomac River site and a plot on the other side of the Inner Loop Freeway, which I had said would also be desirable for the center.

I had originally been persuaded to consider this additional plot in conversation with General Welling and Bill Press. The three of us had agreed it would be advisable to obtain all the excess property on either side of the Inner Loop Freeway, including the Old Observatory, the naval hospital, and several other Navy buildings. Later, however, the chairman of the NCPC advised me that this area was full of rock and too costly to excavate. In addition, the Arlington Memorial Bridge Commission felt that jurisdiction of Constitution Avenue from the Lincoln Memorial to 18th Street should be maintained as a protection for the Lincoln Memorial. If at any time the naval buildings were destroyed, the plan was to use the land as a park to buttress and improve the framework of the Lincoln Memorial. These facts convinced me to withdraw support for the use of this land by the national cultural center.

After my testimony, there was an outcry from supporters of the Mall site. Besides Senator Fulbright, the most vocal of my critics were Representative Thompson; a powerful Georgetown group, the Committee of 100 on the Federal City under Adm. Neill Phillips; George Frain; John Immer, president of the D.C. Federation of Citizens' Associations; and impressario Patrick Hayes. Frain and Immer (and later New Jersey congressman

---

* Mrs. Bacon and I were warm personal friends for nearly half a century, having met in New York when I was president of that state's Young Republicans and she the vice chairman of the Republican State Committee. She was one of the great ladies of Washington. At her splendid home, Bacon House (now used by the Diplomatic and Consular Officers, Retired [DACOR] and supported by the DACOR-Bacon House Foundation), she had organized (with the assistance of my wife, Ann, as secretary) the World Affairs Forum for internationally known speakers, which flourished until her death. Mrs. Bacon was an elegant lady of great taste, very much involved with and supportive of all phases of the arts. I would say her home was like the salons of yesterday we all read about. Artists, including Arthur Rubinstein, stayed there. She wanted to see the proposed national cultural center located on the Potomac, particularly since she had served on the demised D.C. Auditorium Commission that had recommended the Foggy Bottom site.

Foggy Bottom and unrestored Georgetown, about 1950, before construction of the Theodore Roosevelt Bridge and the Inner Loop Freeway. The Rock Creek Golf Club was then located next to the Lincoln Memorial. A decision to place the Center near here, on the site of the old Heurich Brewery, embroiled the trustees in a bitter controversy that lasted for more than eight years.

William B. Widnall) vigorously attacked the Potomac River location for eight years. Officers and directors of the Board of Trade were approached and pressured to change their position. A considerable number of the letters they received were in support of Marjorie Hendricks, whose Watergate Inn occupied a block needed to square out the site.

Senator Fulbright and members of the Senate Public Works Committee recognized the potential for stalemate. Seeking a pragmatic solution, Fulbright, in consultation with Senators McNamara and Chavez, agreed to refer the matter of location to the eight-member Fine Arts Commission.

Under consideration by that commission were four sites owned by the government. As described in the May 20, 1958, letter of the commission's chairman, David E. Finley, to Senator Fulbright, they included (1) the Mall site directly south of the National Gallery of Art; (2) the river site overlooking the Potomac River at 26th Street, Rock Creek and Potomac Parkway, south of New Hampshire Avenue; (3) the Constitution Avenue site of the old naval hospital bounded by 23rd Street on the east, Constitution Avenue on the south, 25th Street on the west, and E Street on the north; and (4) the site of the Old Pension Office building bounded by 4th, 5th, F, and G Streets, Northwest.

At a meeting of the Fine Arts Commission on that same day, I spoke strongly in favor of the Potomac River site. Opponents also spoke, among them Patrick Hayes; Robert Woods Bliss, chairman of the site committee of the Committee of 100; Oscar Cox of the Opera Society of Washington; and George Garrett, president of the Federal City Council.

After the discussions, Finley asked for a consensus of those present. A majority of the interested people at the meeting favored the river site overlooking the Potomac. Consensus was developing for this location because, as Finley wrote in his letter, "others whose first choice was the Mall site also favored the river site in the event the Mall site could not be made available." Finley went on to report that the group advocated that Congress authorize the NCPC to use funds already available to acquire the rest of the land the government did not already own.

On May 22, the commission held a formal meeting and approved the Potomac site. This approval was indicated in a letter to Representative Thompson contained in Senate Report No. 1700, dated June 11, 1958. Senator Fulbright and the Senate Public Works Committee accepted the commission's recommendations, substituting the description of the river site for the one on the Mall that had appeared in the original bills.

There were other changes as the river site came to be accepted. On June 19, 1958, Rep. James G. Fulton (R-Pa.) introduced legislation with new language creating a board of trustees. The board was to be a bureau of the Smithsonian, removed from the jurisdiction of the regents; in accord with the wishes of Smithsonian officials, the center was to be set up as a distinct entity. On the Senate side, Senator Fulbright asked that the names of Alexander Wiley, the senior senator from Wisconsin and the ranking

Republican on the Foreign Affairs Committee, and of Clinton Anderson, the junior senator from New Mexico, be added as cosponsors of the bill. Enhancing support by lining up cosponsors is an accepted tactic. In this case, it proved even more important. Senator Wiley's able administrative assistant, Julius Cahn, helped get the necessary bipartisan support in the Senate.

Also on June 11, 1958, Senator Chavez submitted the report to accompany S. 3335. It outlined the administrative mechanisms necessary to make the center a reality.

> The purpose of S. 3335, as amended, is to establish in the Smithsonian Institution a Board of Trustees of the National Cultural Center, composed of 15 specified Federal officials, members ex officio and 15 General Trustees appointed by the President, to cause to be constructed for the Institution, with funds raised by voluntary contributions, a building to be designated as the National Cultural Center on a site in the District of Columbia bounded by Rock Creek Parkway, New Hampshire Avenue, the proposed Inner Loop Freeway, and the approach to the authorized Theodore Roosevelt Bridge. . . .

> This site and the proposed language changes have the approval of the Commission of Fine Arts, the National Capital Planning Commission, the Board of Commissioners of the District of Columbia, the Bureau of the Budget, the Washington Board of Trade and others. The Committee heartily endorses this amendment to S. 3335.

> The Committee believes that music, art, poetry, drama and dance transcend language barriers and provide a means of communication between people of different nationalities which will permit conveyance to people of other countries some of the basic concepts of the American way of life.

> The Committee is of the opinion that enactment of this legislation will permit careful planning and construction of a National Cultural Center worthy of the City of Washington and of America, and will permit our cultural development to keep pace with our economic and scientific development. It believes that vast public benefits will result in awakening and advancing our artistic,

creative, and cultural development and recommends enactment of this legislation.

Added to the report were comments of the relevant federal and district agencies. On June 20 the Senate unanimously passed S. 3335, with amendments substituting the Potomac River site for the Mall site and creating a board of trustees to oversee the building and operation of the center independently of the Smithsonian. By the time of the vote, there was a great sense of bipartisanship and hope for speedy action in the House.

S. 3335 was sent to the House of Representatives three days later and was referred to the Committee on Public Works. A month later, Senator Fulbright expressed a concern common to center advocates in both parties. "I am hopeful," he said, "that this bill will not be lost in the legislative shuffle during the closing days of the 85th Congress."

He was not alone in that hope. Few in Congress and even fewer in the press thought there was time remaining for the bill to clear. Adjourn-

'The arts are a vital part of human experience. In the eyes of posterity, the success of the United States as a civilized society will be largely judged by the creative activities of its citizens in art, architecture, literature, music, and the sciences."

Goals for Americans
Report of the President's Commission on National Goals, 1960, p.9.

ment was tentatively scheduled for August 9, and there was serious doubt that it could even be brought to the House floor. Such might well have been the case had it not been for Rep. Robert Jones (D-Ala.), chairman of a subcommittee of the House Committee on Public Works to which the bill had been referred. Promising me that "the Center bill will pass before adjournment," he extended the meeting of his committee until August 5 to make sure that H.R. 13017 would be heard.

Gratifyingly, hearings opened on August 1. The first witness was Senator Wiley, whose remarks are worth quoting:

> The fact that the president of the United States saw fit, in these busy days, to send a special message endorsing this center to the chairman of the full House Public Works Committee is proof of the significance with which this bill is regarded in the executive branch. I can hardly add in detail to what the president has said on the importance of the center to our nation.
>
> The people of the District of Columbia do want this cultural center. Man does not live by bread alone, you know, and we certainly need evidence to the world that we stand by that concept. . . .
>
> America needs [this national cultural center] as a beacon to the free world. Let the best of American and foreign performing artists appear in this great center in the years up ahead.
>
> I say this as a senior member of the Foreign Relations Committee. It ill behooves the capital of the greatest nation in the world to lack a center of this type, here in the city where more than 80 foreign embassies, accredited to us, note this very serious shortcoming in our national cultural endeavors. Why not henceforth put our best foot forward to the world?
>
> This legislation is basically a green light for private enterprise to function. It is, as you know, private enterprise which will raise the funds to construct this center. I do not have the slightest doubt that under appropriate leadership there will come forth ample voluntary contributions from the 48 states, from people of means and people of more modest resources, so as to achieve this great goal.

Two themes seemed to recur in statements supporting the legislation. One was a growing sense of the position of the United States in the world. The other was that the time had come to fulfill a historic mandate. Representative Thompson's remarks reflected both. Earlier, committee chairman Charles A. Buckley (D-N.Y.) had received a letter from President Eisenhower, drafted by presidential assistant Bryce Harlow, which I requested from Sherman Adams. Referring to this letter, Thompson said:

> [T]his is not the first time President Eisenhower has urged the Congress to actively support the fine arts. You will recall his statements in his 1955 message on the state of the Union that [with respect to] "advancement of the various activities which will make our civilization endure and flourish, the federal government should do more to give official recognition to the importance of the arts and other cultural activities."
>
> In saying this the president was simply carrying on in the spirit of a great and basic tradition of the United States which has marked all branches of the federal government through all the years since the birth of this nation. In his first annual address to Congress on January 8, 1790, President George Washington said, "You will agree . . . that there is nothing which can better deserve our patronage than the promotion of science and literature. Whether this desirable object will be best promoted by affording aids to seminaries of learning already established, by the institution of a national university, or by any other expedients, will be worthy of the place in the deliberations of the legislature."
>
> Another time, George Washington said, "The prosperity of our country is closely connected with our improvement in the useful arts," and "the arts and sciences essential to the prosperity of the state and to the ornament and happiness of human life have a primary claim to the encouragement of every lover of his country and mankind."
>
> President Washington commissioned Major Pierre L'Enfant in 1789 to plan the federal city as a cultural and civic center of the new United States. Indeed, the Founding Fathers saw the nation's capital as a new Athens, a city of light and learning.

I, too, reflected very much the themes of the time. In my own testimony, I had said, in speaking for the Board of Trade:

Events in recent years, including the establishment of the international cultural exchange program and the emphasis on culture at the Brussels Fair, demonstrate a growing acceptance of the thesis that in any cold war competition we cannot afford the Soviets to outdo us in the cultural field any more than we can in ballistic missiles.

In my humble opinion the inadequacy of cultural facilities in Washington is the one major area of emphasis on the arts that has been neglected in our efforts to match the Communists. As appears likely, our cultural exchange with Russia will continue to increase in magnitude, and we must be prepared to afford the great Soviet and other foreign attractions a highly suitable palace for their performances in our nation's capital.

I was delighted to read that none other than the president of the United States found time in these critical days to address a letter to the distinguished chairman of this committee advocating passage of the legislation you now have under consideration. The president is entirely correct in noting the inadequacies of cultural facilities in our nation's capital, and I trust that this committee will act to meet these pressing needs of our fair city.

As stated in the beginning of my remarks, I am here as an official spokesman of the Washington Board of Trade, and we take pride in the fact that the Board of Trade took the lead in urging the selection of the site which is provided for in the bill we are considering. We arrived at the selection of the site after long and thoughtful attention to every facet of the problem and only after complete consultation and cooperation with the officials of the District of Columbia government. . . .

[The board of directors of the Board of Trade . . . has] over the years stood by and encouraged progress made in the nation's capital. . . . Our membership, which is over 7,000, is enthusiastically in favor of this project.

The most important thing I can say is that prior to the hearings in the Senate Subcommittee, there was a question of site.

If that is not decided at this session, it might be impossible to obtain this particular site.

Fortunately, both the bill and myself had the right kind of support. Richard Sullivan, counsel to the House committee, was consistently reliable on legislative strategy, but as we got down to the wire, nobody figured more importantly than Representative Jones of Alabama. As chairman of the subcommittee responsible for the Smithsonian and other public works, Jones had a broad vision of Washington's future; he did more for the District of Columbia, and received less credit, than any other congressman in modern times.

August 5 was the last day of hearings, and it was then that Jones's leadership proved crucial. With adjournment closing in, the only way H.R. 13017 could be brought to the floor was by a suspension of the House rules, and to do that would take a two-thirds vote. Jones chose to pursue a good but dangerous strategy. On August 22, he brought the bill to the floor and moved to suspend the rules, which meant that no further amendments would be permitted. The Speaker asked for a second. Then, there being no objection, Rep. H. R. Gross (R-Iowa) made a point of order that a quorum was not present. The Speaker agreed, whereupon Jones moved for a roll call. After 321 answered to their names, a quorum was declared present. Jones then yielded five minutes to Rep. James Wright, Jr. (D-Texas), who reviewed the bill's provisions and asked for an immediate vote. A strong center supporter and a real "ball carrier" for the legislation that created it, Jim Wright would later become majority leader and Speaker of the House.

During the relatively brief floor debate, Thompson recalled the pioneering work of Carroll Kearns. Jones, emphasizing the bipartisan spirit that had surrounded the entire effort, made note of the contributions of Senators Fulbright, Anderson, and Wiley, and also acknowledged the support of Vice President Nixon. Most of the other remarks were similarly favorable to passage, although there were some conservatives who thought it inappropriate for the federal government to become directly involved in the arts, and a few who questioned the cost to federal taxpayers. In response to this last point, Jones reiterated in closing that the center would be financed with voluntary contributions: "This is a bill that will not cost the federal taxpayers a red cent and will provide a center that is badly needed to show to the world the American culture of which we are so justly proud." Jones also reaffirmed the use of Capper-Crampton Act monies.*

After some last-minute delaying tactics by our perennial critic H. R. Gross, the Speaker asked if the House would suspend the rules and pass the bill, as earlier amended. After another call for a quorum, with two-thirds of the House voting, the bill passed: 261 yes, 55 no, 113 not voting.

Those of us who had worked so long and hard were jubilant. I was pleased particularly to have addressed the site issue as I did, for in retrospect it seems clear that it was only with its resolution that events began to turn in our favor. Since its completion, the National Air and Space Museum has proved to be the most popular museum in the nation, averaging 9 million visitors a year. If we had not been able to break the stalemate over the Mall site, perhaps neither it nor the Kennedy Center would exist today.

Relieved and exhilarated, I remember looking forward to the work ahead. What I didn't know was that eight long years of controversy were yet to come before the land would be assembled.

ON SEPTEMBER 2, 1958, while on summer vacation in Newport, R.I., President Eisenhower signed the National Cultural Center Act.** His message was clear, succinct, and prophetic:

> The cultural center belongs to the entire country. The challenge of its development offers to each of us a noble opportunity to add to the aesthetic and spiritual fabric of America.

So true. The National Cultural Center Act provided that its board of trustees:

1. Present classical and contemporary music, opera, drama, dance, and poetry from this and other countries;
2. Present lectures and other programs;
3. Develop programs for children and youth and the elderly (and for

---

* The Capper-Crampton Act (46 Stat. 842) provided funds for parks, parkways, and playgrounds in the District of Columbia.

** P.L. 85-874, 85th Cong., 72 Stat. 1698, September 2, 1958.

other age groups as well) in such arts designed specifically for their participation, education, and recreation;

4. Provide facilities for other civic activities at the National Cultural Center for the Performing Arts.

Thus, in the broadest language possible was the platform laid for realization of the Center's mission: to present artistic programming of the highest quality, to serve as a national focus for the performing arts in America, and to reach the widest feasible audience.*

On January 29, 1959, as Section 2(b) of the statute directed, the president appointed 15 general trustees to hold office for 10 years under an originally staggered system of 2-, 4-, 6-, 8-, and 10-year terms. I was one of them and proud to be in their company.**

In addition, the law named as ex officio members 15 representatives of the executive and legislative branches, one of whom was Arthur S. Flemming, the then secretary of Health, Education, and Welfare.** At the first meeting of the board, held at the White House on March 13, 1959, Secretary Flemming was elected chairman, L. Corrin Strong vice chairman, and Daniel Bell treasurer. On the same day an Executive Committee meeting was convened in Secretary Flemming's office. In addition to the board's officers, the committee consisted of Leonard Carmichael, secretary of the Smithsonian Institution; David E. Finley, chairman of the Fine Arts Commission; and myself as general counsel. Early in April the Center was assigned official headquarters at 718 Jackson Place, a federal government building on Lafayette Square.

Simultaneously at the little White House in Augusta, Ga., President Eisenhower appointed the Advisory Committee on the Arts** to assist him and the Center as needed.

With bylaws approved on April 27, 1959, the board of trustees amplified the original objectives:

> The National Cultural Center is destined to stand as a monument to America's cultural maturity and to her realization that the

* Five-and-a-half years later, on January 29, 1964, another section was added to the act to rename the Center the John F. Kennedy Center for the Performing Arts as the "sole living memorial in the Nation's Capital" to the assassinated president.

** For roster of members see appendix, page 202 and 203.

conquest of material things cannot stand the test of time until they find fruition in the realm of the mind and soul. The peoples of 50 sovereign states, sharing a love for political freedoms of self-government, seek in the creation of a cultural center a concrete expression of their common attachment to the arts.

That same day, Jarrold A Kieffer, Flemming's assistant at HEW, was elected secretary of the board; Mrs. J. C. Cantrell, Jr., assistant secretary; and Paul J. Seltzer, assistant treasurer.

One of our first tasks was to choose an architect, and for that purpose, Strong and I had an early meeting with officials and architects of the Lincoln Center in New York. Their advice was to select only one architect because "too many cooks in the kitchen spoil the broth." Alice (Mrs. L. Corrin) Strong, daughter of distinguished New York architect Alexander Buel Trowbridge, participated in the selection.

At a meeting of the board on June 23, 1959, Edward Durell Stone was selected as architect-adviser to develop a concept for the project along with appropriate plans. Trained at Harvard and the Massachusetts Institute of Technology, Stone was a recognized scholar of architectural history. He held a professorship at Yale, and his genius, artistry, imagination, and lyrical eloquence did much to enhance the stature of his profession. His expensive ideas and tastes, however, often led to budget problems.

Arthur S. Flemming, in 1959 secretary of the Department of Health, Education, and Welfare, was the first chairman of the Center's board of trustees.

Architect Edward Durell Stone's first plans called for a "people's shrine to culture" 100 feet high and 180 feet in diameter. The entrance to the grand salon would have been from the Potomac River, and Stone envisaged patrons arriving by barge. His clamshell design, substantially revised after Roger Stevens's arrival as chairman, inspired Italian architect Luigi Moretti to use a complementary romantic style for the neighboring Watergate complex.

In designing the Center he placed his emphasis on the Potomac River, referring to it as "an idyllic setting." He envisioned taking advantage of the natural majesty of the waterside location, much like the Houses of Parliament in London and the Louvre in Paris. Romantically, he pictured galleys in all their glory entering this palace of the arts from the river.

Several months after selecting Stone, on October 31, a joint meeting of the board of trustees and the Advisory Committee was held in accordance with Section 2(c) of the statute, which provided for the appointment of associated organizations to assist the board.* Stone and his associates submitted building plans and cost estimates at that meeting. Depending on

* For roster of members see appendix, page 203.

options that we could only vaguely identify, we were told that the cost would range anywhere from $30 million to $70 million. A month before, our financial report showed $1,067,000 in pledges.

A month later, having reviewed the proposals, the Executive Committee confirmed the selection of Stone as architect. That behind us, we were organized and ready for Phase Two.

3

HITS AND MISSES:
The First Design and Early Fund Raising

What, then, did it take to create this modern shrine to culture? Reviewing the 13 years from 1958 to 1971, I cannot overlook the strife and struggle. But it was also a time in which I had the opportunity to associate with men and women of distinctive vision and genuine accomplishment. What remains with me most is the fact that we surmounted what seemed at the time to be daunting problems. One was the difficulty of developing a "boomerang"* site of 7.5 government-owned acres, unusable in its original form, into a 17.5-acre plot; this prompted a bitter quarrel over the site that lasted for eight years. Further, there was the controversial grand concept and design by Edward Durell Stone, the drawn-out dispute over Stage IV of the Watergate buildings, and the debate over traffic patterns for entering and exiting the Center. We also confronted larger but less tangible issues, such as creating a national image for the Center rather than a parochial one.

The biggest problem, however, was fund raising. During the last year of the Eisenhower administration, the board of trustees got to work. The Center was financially in the black (though not by very much) because of the generosity of L. Corrin Strong, a founding trustee, executive vice chairman, chairman, and chairman emeritus. Strong was a former ambassador to Norway, where he had been unusually popular, and he was a prudent philanthropist. His contribution to the Center of more than a million dollars paid administrative costs and salaries and also permitted

---

* So-called because of its shape.

the acquisition of real estate. His wife, Alice, shared in his work on the Center and was a substantial donor, the most visible of her gifts being the trees and shrubs that surround the Center today.

Interest in the project continued apace with the new administration. Strong had the foresight to facilitate good relations between the Eisenhower and Kennedy teams, and the transition was easy, warm, and thoroughly professional. President Kennedy, while serving as senator from Massachusetts, had supported a national cultural center. Once in the White House he proved to be a man of his word. Two months after taking office, he expressed a personal interest, asking for detailed reports about our progress. It was his policy from the beginning to issue all announcements about the Center as official White House press releases, thereby giving us a national audience and the imprimatur of the presidency. Key members of his staff, particularly Fred Dutton, were in regular communication with Center officials. A main point of contact was Robert Richman, president of the Institute of Contemporary Arts and a member of our Advisory Committee. Jarrold A. Kieffer, the secretary of the board of trustees, prepared and dispatched staff papers.

On January 18, 1961, as one of his last acts before leaving office, President Eisenhower had written a letter to Congress requesting legislation to enlarge the Foggy Bottom site. On March 2, in the same spirit of advocacy, Kennedy wrote a letter to Vice President Lyndon B. Johnson and House Speaker Rayburn with a more specific request—that the government acquire three parcels of land needed to meet the specifications of the architect's first plans. Of all the actions he took in the early days, however, the most significant emerged from his tagging for top priority the problem of financing. Estimates based on the original design had put the project's cost as high as $85 million. To raise a sum of this magnitude entirely from the private sector seemed a hopeless task. After all, the nation's capital had no industry, and most people at the time thought of the Center as a local Washington project.

President Kennedy understood the problem and was looking for seven top-level national figures to fill the vacancies on the board of trustees, as well as a strong chairman who would focus on raising funds from the private sector. To serve as chairman, he turned to Roger L. Stevens, a leading businessman and real estate developer with a keen interest in the performing arts. Stevens had produced more than 200 theatrical productions on Broadway, many of them cited among the 10 best plays of the year. He had also been president of the Producers Theatre and of the New Dramatists Committee, and a member of the board of the Metropolitan Opera Company. What's more, he was a successful fund raiser, having served as national finance chairman of the Democratic party and as treasurer of the Adlai Stevenson campaign. His business activities, largely in real estate, included some of the nation's most important projects; he was, for instance, head of the syndicate that purchased the Empire State Building in 1951.

Stevens was uniquely qualified in background and character, and abundantly equipped with talent, skill, vision, guts, and fortitude for this difficult project. I served with him for many years and can speak with firsthand knowledge about his shrewdness, fearlessness, and gambling instincts. He was, in the best sense, a successful operator. He agreed to give, and did give, the project his full time. Moreover, except for expenses and a car and driver, he gave it without compensation.

Named with him on September 3, 1961, were two new trustees: Mary (Mrs. Albert D.) Lasker and K. LeMoyne Billings. Mary Lasker is an outstanding woman, distinguished both as a philanthropist and as a patron, collector, and dealer in the fine arts, especially the old and modern French masters. As early as 1943 she was busy with planting programs to enhance the parks of New York City, and she was one of Lady Bird Johnson's most active cohorts in the Beautification Program of the sixties. Her work in the fields of health and medicine was even more impressive. Often called "The First Lady in Health," she lobbied tirelessly for the National Institutes of Health and did much to revive and rebuild the American Cancer Society. In 1942 she and her husband founded the Albert and Mary Lasker Foundation, which makes awards for contributions to medical research and public health administration; since 1950 the foundation has also recognized achievements in medical journalism. At the time she joined our board, she was a trustee of both New York University and Long Island University. In recognition of her distinguished public service she received the Presidential Medal of Freedom from President Johnson on January 29, 1969. Twenty years later, on April 21, 1989, President George Bush awarded her the Congressional Gold Medal.

LeMoyne Billings was a lifelong friend and schoolmate of President Kennedy. Eunice Kennedy Shriver once said that of the 10 friends closest to the president, Lem was at the top of the list. He was a gentleman, an activist, and an invaluable asset to the board, serving as liaison between the Center and the president. It was Lem who, with the Kennedy family, later arranged for the conversion of the National Cultural Center into the John F. Kennedy Center for the Performing Arts as a living memorial to the fallen president. He was also chairman of the memorial committee that recommended the Robert Berks sculpture of JFK for the Grand Foyer, and he worked with Arthur Schlesinger to choose the appropriate inscriptions of Kennedy's famous words for the exterior marble. And it was Lem who arranged through the White House for GSA to be our agent for design and construction, a stroke of genius that I came to appreciate fully only when we began to establish and weave our way through the shifting, often perplexing, and sometimes fragile terms of relationship with contractors.

Early in November 1961, the remaining vacancies on the board of trustees were filled, and representatives of national organizations were added as members of the Advisory Committee. On November 14, at a meeting of the trustees at the White House, Roger Stevens formally took over as chairman. An hour later the trustees joined the Advisory Committee in a meeting at which the major subject was the need to raise funds from the private sector. At 12:45 p.m., President Kennedy joined us and, after reaffirming his commitment to carry on the work begun by President Eisenhower, went on to say:

> Last night we were particularly fortunate to have one of the most distinguished artists in the world [a reference to Pablo Casals's performance at the White House], and I am hopeful it will not be necessary always to have a special stage put in the White House for Shakespeare or for a special hearing for a distinguished musician, but that in Washington here we can have a great cultural center which expresses the interest of the people of this country in the most basic desire of mankind.
>
> This is a most important national responsibility, and I can assure you that, if you will be willing to help, . . . this administration will give it every possible support. We face many hazards, all of which you have been through before in your own communities, many

difficulties in not only building it but maintaining it, but I am confident that we can do it. I think it is an issue that we put face forward to the world.

In the early days of his chairmanship, Stevens turned to questions of architecture. Edward Durell Stone's plans for the Center were for a building of clamshell design that would extend over the banks of the Potomac River, an imaginative concept of palatial grandeur. Reflective of this first design is today's Watergate complex. It is round because the Italian architect, Luigi Moretti, followed Stone's concept and designed Watergate to be harmonious.

At the eighth meeting of the board of trustees, on January 19, 1962, architectural planning was the major subject. Contemplating Stone's grand design, we considered building the Center in three phases, but as an experienced developer, Stevens believed the design too costly and thought it should be substantially revised or abandoned. Some of the features, such as grand staircases and large open spaces, were expensive and impractical. Stevens advocated a more utilitarian design (at half the price) that would still provide major facilities and maintain high aesthetic standards. With the president's agreement, he went back to the architect. Stone proved flexible and redesigned the Center, incorporating all three performance halls into one multilevel building. The cost estimate was thereby reduced significantly to $31 million, which then became our new fund-raising goal.

Aware that the scope and purpose of the project required a national effort, President Kennedy issued a proclamation on October 15, 1962, designating the period from November 26 through December 2, 1962, as "National Cultural Center Week." Highlight of the week was a television gala, "An American Pageant of the Arts," broadcast on November 29 in 75 cities and originating at a dinner hosted by the president in the National Guard Armory. In the spirit of the occasion, modest donation buffet dinners were held at various other sites around the city, including the campuses of American, Georgetown, Catholic, and Howard universities in the District and the University of Maryland across the District line in College Park.

At the armory, President Kennedy opened the telecast by recognizing dignitaries in attendance. Then, by remote pickup to Augusta, Ga., he

The national fund-raising drive was kicked off on November 29, 1962, with an appearance by President and Mrs. Kennedy on a closed circuit television show seen in 75 cities.

turned to his predecessor and said, "We are particularly pleased to have as our guest tonight . . . the man under whose administration this project was started and who has given it wholehearted support—ladies and gentlemen, General Eisenhower."

The former president then made the following speech:

> Mrs. Eisenhower and I are privileged this evening to spend this particular night in charming Augusta, and with such company and with you to witness the great exhibition of American performing arts that we have seen on television. To each of the artists we give our sincere thanks and expression of our great appreciation.

> Mamie and I lived in Washington a long time—long before 1953. In those days, it was quite rare that any heads of state or heads of government came to Washington. But in the later years Washington became the political crossroads of the world. It was visited by kings and queens, presidents and prime ministers—and in the future it will be so visited even much more frequently—and in their train save come many others, and they have learned much about America that they did not know before.

> Many years ago when we were in Europe, it was not too rare at all to hear our country spoken of as another colony. When a European spoke of coming to America, he would say, "we are going out there next year to see you people," and it was in sort of a conde-

scending tone. But as these visitors have come to Washington and have been privileged to go and see our broad lands, our great cities, our humming factories, and learn more about this great country, they begin to appreciate also that there was here a culture that had been growing and developing over the decades, and it was a culture that in all its forms deserved the respect of all the world. So, finally, in the later years when I was acting as the chief executive, the idea was born that in Washington there should be a center of culture—an American center of culture to which all the artists of the United States could repair, which would be sort of an artistic mecca—indeed, that would be open to visitors from every land. In all of the arts, then, people would come to see in sort of a nutshell what America was capable of showing, not only in her factories, in her productivity, in her great strength, her wealth, and in her prosperity, her great roads and highways, but . . . in the arts and in those things that appeal to all that is spiritually aesthetic to the senses of man.

So I think this dinner tonight, starting off for the material side of the development of this great culture, is something that each of us can take some pride in participating in. I do hope that each of us that has heard and seen this performance this evening will take some inspiration from it and try to be a part—himself and herself—in making this Center a true mecca for artists—one that will give everybody who visits Washington, whether from our own country or from the four corners of the world, a true appreciation, a better appreciation of America.

President Kennedy then continued,

[W]e are glad to be the guests of honor of the representatives of much of the finest in American culture and much of the finest in American life. . . .

Thomas Jefferson wrote that the one thing which from the heart he envied certain other nations . . . was their art, [and] he spoke from a deep understanding of the enduring sources of national greatness and national achievement.

But our culture and art do not speak to America alone. To the extent that artists struggle to express beauty in form and color and sound, to the extent that they write about man's struggle with nature

President Kennedy wanted his predecessor's approval of Stone's revised plan, so on September 19, 1962, officials of the Center journeyed to the Eisenhower farm in Gettysburg, Pa. Heading the delegation were Roger Stevens (center) and Amb. L. Corrin Strong, executive vice president and a major donor.

Mrs. Eisenhower greets the author, Mrs. Strong, and Mrs. Stevens.

Architect Edward Durell Stone shows the former president and Mrs. Eisenhower his model of the National Cultural Center. Prior to this Washington commission, Stone was primarily known for his design of the U.S. Embassy building in New Delhi, and for his design (with Philip Goodwin) of the Museum of Modern Art in New York City.

or society or himself, to that extent they strike a responsive chord in all humanity.

Produced by Robert Saudek, the gala gave us a dazzling sampler of American drama, music, and dance, the artists appearing in live performances telecast from stages in Washington, Chicago, New York, and Los Angeles. Among them were Pablo Casals, Dorothy Kirsten, Marian Anderson, Van Cliburn, Benny Goodman, Danny Kaye, Maria Tallchief, Bob Newhart, Harry Belafonte, Yo-Yo Ma, Fredric March, and the National Symphony Orchestra. The event gave coast-to-coast media attention to the Center as a national bipartisan project, and it was a great critical success. Unfortunately, it brought in less than a half million dollars, whereas Stevens had expected it to raise millions.

Another artistic but less than financial success was *Creative America*, a handsome volume of photographs and essays published shortly after Kennedy's death. The book was conceived as an elegant fund-raising premium for the Center, and it has since become something of a collector's item. "When man creates, he is affirming his individuality and his humanity," the editors said in a prefatory note. "This book, like the National Cultural Center, is dedicated to that spirit." And its contents were indeed evocative of that spirit, consisting of short eloquent statements by the three U.S. presidents living during the time of its preparation, and by such distinguished writers as James Baldwin, Robert Frost, John Ciardi, Mark Van Doren, and Louis Kronenberger. The intent had been to pay for the first run with advertising from American industry solicited at the rate of $15,000 a page. This could have meant an impressive yield for the Center since we would be getting all proceeds from book sales over manufacturing and marketing costs. The book went to press, however, with no more than 11 advertising pages, and sales were so few that to my best recollection whatever we received was inconsequential.

More successful was a special recording of music played by the service bands. This was a complicated arrangement, requiring protracted negotiations among the Pentagon, the Radio Corporation of America, and the musicians' union. Roger Stevens and I spent much time getting the record produced. Jarrold Kieffer and my campaign assistant, Major Helen Roy, were also involved. For the first time the music of the four U.S. military bands—Army, Navy, Air Force, and Marines—was recorded for sale to the public, with all profits going to the National Cultural Center. The records were released by RCA in May of 1963 and generated more than $120,000 in less than a year.

Stevens devoted much time in 1962-63 to the Center's finances, always with a creative, businesslike approach. A good example was his plan to use revenues from parking to retire the debt incurred to pay for the underground garage. Toward this end, Billings developed an understanding with Secretary of Interior Stewart Udall to the effect that the $14 million needed for the garage could be borrowed from the government—to be repaid, we hoped, over several years—and thereby deducted from the total cost to be raised by contributions. Thus, the $31 million fund-raising goal represented the "superstructure."*

President Kennedy was aware of this understanding. When he met with American business leaders at the White House on October 8, 1963, he used the $31 million figure as the goal.

Two months later, at the Executive Committee meeting on December 4, Stevens and I explained that while the Center needed $31 million for the building of the superstructure, there were two additional expenditures to be considered. First was the land for the site, much of it still in private hands to be acquired by the NCPC at a cost of $3 million in appropriated funds. Second was the 1,500-car underground parking garage, the cost of which had not been included in our set goal of $31 million. (Independent expert surveys indicated that the parking facility could be self-liquidating with a net yearly income of $600,000.) Thus, adding the $14 million estimated for the garage to the established goal of $31 million brought the architect's preliminary estimate for total construction costs to approximately $45 million. We agreed that requests for funds be based on this total cost and on contingencies of another $5 million, making for a budget of $50 million.

In addition to enlisting the president's assistance, Stevens had also turned to Jacqueline Kennedy, who, on February 24, 1962, agreed to serve as honorary chairman of the fund-raising campaign. A few months later, on April 18, Mrs. Dwight D. Eisenhower joined her as honorary cochairman.

* In plans for fund raising, the performance halls were referred to as the "superstructure." Below this plaza level was the "substructure"—that is, the three levels of parking.

Then, using White House relationships, Stevens set up numerous fund-raising committees. Mrs. Kennedy's mother, Janet (Mrs. Hugh D.) Auchincloss, agreed to serve as chairman of the Greater Washington Committee, assuming responsibility for raising $7.5 million.

There were also other District efforts, these directed at the local community. Robert C. Baker, chairman of the board of American Security and Trust Company, organized a Special Gifts Campaign Committee to solicit donations of $1,000 and over. I chaired the General Campaign Committee to solicit donations in amounts up to $1,000, and toward that end I concentrated on the area's universities, businesses, labor unions, professional organizations, fraternal orders, schools, and the military. When I referred to this as an effort to raise "nickels and dimes," Marie McNair picked up the phrase in her well-read column in the *Washington Post* and gave us some very productive publicity. In another local effort, authorized by the Board of Education, approximately $20,000 was raised by schoolchildren through paper and scrap drives. This was more than the total amount raised from the 30,000 Pentagon employees (except for a special gift from Secretary of Defense Robert S. McNamara).

John S. Gleason, Jr., administrator of the Veterans Administration, served as federal campaign chairman for Washington-area government employee contributions, including those of the armed forces. He designated his deputy, S. William Melidosian of Philadelphia, an imaginative and vigorous activist, to spearhead this difficult campaign, which raised more than $118,000.

On the national level, Stevens appointed a Presidents Business Committee under the chairmanship of Ernest R. Breech, a trustee and former chairman of the Ford Motor Company, who was then director and chairman of Trans World Airlines. Many prominent businessmen in the United States agreed to serve on this committee. In the early 1960s it was extremely difficult to obtain funds for the arts from corporations, and the committee was able to raise only about half of its $6 million goal, in sharp contrast to the millions of dollars now contributed by industry.

The president appointed Edgar M. Bronfman, president of Joseph E. Seagram and Sons, Inc., as trustee and also made him chairman of the Seat Endowment Committee. Individuals and organizations were invited to endow a permanent seat in one of the Center's three halls for a contribution of $1,000. A bronze plaque would be affixed to the back of the seat. Bronfman's efforts brought in about $23,000.

LIKE MOST OF THE THINGS WE DID for the Center in these early days, fund raising was a team affair, so much so that whenever somebody asks me, "Who did that?" or "Who was the first to come up with that idea?" or "Who deserves credit for this?" I often find it impossible to single out an individual. I cannot, for instance, truly remember who first suggested that we undertake a systematic campaign to solicit contributions of building materials, art objects, and furnishings, or who first thought about asking foreign governments for such gifts. Roger Stevens, Mary Lasker, Lem Billings, and I met often, and our meetings usually produced at least one brainstorm. Anyway, at some point early in 1962, Stone worked up a "laundry list" (you name it—it had on it everything from chandeliers to aluminum ingots to plumbing fixtures to theater seats), and we began a discreet approach to manufacturers and suppliers, both here and abroad. Because in my law practice I represented a lot of other countries, I was put in charge of foreign gifts.

During one of our meetings early in 1963, I asked Billings about the possibility of a gift of marble from Italy. He immediately took the idea to President Kennedy, who was scheduled to meet in Rome with President Antonio Segni in June. Kennedy agreed to talk with Segni about it, and in preparation, Stone drafted a memorandum estimating the quantities of marble needed. Billings took the memorandum with him when he accompanied the president to Italy that summer. On his return on July 5, President Kennedy announced from the White House that Italy was making a magnificent gift of marble to the Center. Just like that!

But getting the marble was not as easy as I make it sound. Although we assumed the gift included enough marble for both the interior and exterior, no amount had been specified in the government's pledge. The Italian government changed hands so often that it took a great deal of lobbying and the better part of two years to get Segni's pledge through the Italian Chamber of Deputies. In September 1964, my wife and I met in Paris with the secretary general of NATO, Manlio Brosio, a former ambassador to the United States, a well-respected official, and an old friend of mine. He agreed to take all steps necessary to convert the pledge into a commitment. In addition, I conferred with Sen. John O. Pastore (D-R.I.), who contacted friends in the Italian Parliament, and I got in touch with New York Supreme Court Justice Victor Anfuso, formerly a powerful member of Congress. He had a strong relationship with Prime Minister Aldo Moro, who had lived in Anfuso's congressional district during the Fascist regime. Moro turned out to be our chief ball carrier. Mary Lasker played an important role, too. She communicated with Amb. Egidio Ortona, who was then in the foreign ministry. Lem Billings went to Italy twice with authorizations from the White House and from Harry C. McPherson, Jr., assistant secretary of State and an ex officio trustee of the Center; he met with the minister of culture and others in order to expedite action by the Italian Parliament. Vice President Hubert Humphrey wrote to Giuseppe Lupus, the under secretary for foreign affairs. Italian ambassador Sergio Fenolatea and his former aide, Cesare Gnoli, who was then assigned to the foreign ministry in Rome, were particularly helpful in arranging meetings with Italian leaders.

On May 25, 1965, I received a telegram from our ambassador in Rome, G. Frederick Reinhardt, via the State Department. Parliament, he informed me, had authorized 400 million lire—the equivalent of $600,000—for marble for the Center. It had not said, however, which of several companies was to supply us; that particular choice, which had some interesting diplomatic overtones, would be up to us. So, anticipating some months of bargaining, I worked out a transfer of the funds and deposited them in Washington's Riggs National Bank.

The American Marble Institute raised a number of objections to this gift, and senators and representatives from U.S. marble-producing states (Ohio, Vermont, Tennessee, Georgia, and Alabama) communicated their objections to the White House. At the institute's urging, domestic companies refused to work on the Italian marble, so it was necessary to have it "polished and honed" at the source. This increased our cost, but the suppliers were happy to do it. When we then asked the institute if they would give us any marble for water fountains, rest rooms, and the plazas, they said no.

In the colors and dimensions that Stone specified, the marble came from three sources, all in the Carrara mountains. The most important

Three different quarries, all located on the Canal Grande in the vicinity of Carrara, supplied the 3,000 tons of marble donated by the Italian government. The exterior marble was taken from the same Mt. Altissimo quarries that provided the stone for Michelangelo's famous works.

marble—that for the exterior—was produced at the Henreaux quarry at Mt. Altissimo, the highest point in the Carraras. Henreaux's white marble is of rare purity, the hardest in the world and of sculpture quality. It was used in Michelangelo's great works—David, the Pieta, and Moses. (It was, by the way, at Mt. Altissimo that the motion picture, *The Agony and the Ecstasy*, based on Irving Stone's fictionalized biography of Michelangelo, was filmed.) It can also be found in the contemporary sculptures of Henry Moore and Isamu Noguchi.

Stone's original specifications presented a problem. As generous as the Italians had been, they had not given us enough money to pay for all the marble at the 8-inch depth of cut his plans required. The Henreaux company's answer was to bond a 7/8-inch slice of marble, called a "skin," to an 8-inch slab of concrete. Each slab was drilled on its underside, allowing it to be grabbed by small steel hooks, which served the same function as steel reinforcement rods in concrete walls. The technique had been worked out by the University of Pisa and had withstood the test of time in Europe. It had never been tried in the United States, however, and before the method could be approved for the Center, it had to be passed by both GSA and the Bureau of Standards, which brought in a specialist from Chicago to test it.

After the technique had been found eminently acceptable, Henreaux shipped us the slabs, each one labeled by an ingenious engineer at the quarry to identify its location on the finished building. The slabs were then fixed onto "coffins" of concrete made by a subcontractor in Maryland. To supervise the installation—a technical miracle if there ever was one— Henreaux sent one of its chief engineers to Washington.

As evidenced by the number of overseas contributions to the completed Center, the response to our solicitations was extraordinary—and probably unprecedented. Each gift, however, presented a monumental legal issue. The Center, built for the Smithsonian Institution, was not your ordinary federal facility. This made accepting foreign gifts more difficult than if they had been donated by one government to another. With respect to the governments of Denmark, Germany, Italy, Japan, and Norway, we exchanged diplomatic notes with their ambassadors in Washington, and their gifts were used for matching congressionally appropriated funds (see chap. 6). When the notes were presented to the General Accounting Office (GAO), we included acknowledgments by the secretary of State on behalf of the Kennedy Center. Such notes and acknowledgments were customary ways of presenting gifts of foreign governments to the United States. Charles A. Bevans, ably assisted by Frederick T. Teal, passed on all treaties at State and was of great help in our dealings with foreign governments, as

Roger Stevens, Amb. Sergio Fenolatea, and I at an on-site ceremony marking acceptance of Italy's gift. Speeches had been interrupted by overflying jets, prompting Stevens to volunteer that the engineers had pledged to insulate the interior from aircraft noise: "If they fail, I'm going to throw the architect into the Potomac and jump in after him—but not to save him."

was the acting assistant secretary for public affairs, Arthur W. Hummel.

I started negotiations with the ambassador of Ireland, who paved the way for Billings to deal with the Waterford Crystal Company. The result was a gift from Ireland presented by the visiting prime minister, Sean LeMass, to President Kennedy on October 18, 1963. The gift of crystal chandeliers and four crystal sconces was valued at $35,000. It is in the South Opera Lounge, also known as the Golden Circle.

In response to Norway's offer of a gift of crystal chandeliers for the Concert Hall, negotiations began in July 1964 with Amb. Hans Engen, with whom I had cordial relations. In the beginning, Stone was lukewarm to the offer, feeling that Norwegian glassworks were an unknown commodity. Engen told me that, on the contrary, Norway had been famous for 350 years for its glass sculptures and chandeliers. Once Stone was convinced, negotiations proceeded and, after Stone's approval of the design, were consummated. In 1971, King Olaf V of Norway visited Washington, and I was invited to escort him on a tour of the Kennedy Center for a look at his country's gift. By a lucky coincidence, Leonard Bernstein happened to be in the Concert Hall that day rehearsing his *Mass*, which he would introduce at the Center's opening a few days later.

J. & L. Lobmeyr of Vienna is one of the most distinguished glass and chandelier manufacturers in the world. Stone knew that Austria had been on my client list for years—actually, since 1952—and urged me to negotiate a gift of chandeliers for the Opera House. Everyone at the Austrian embassy was receptive; Amb. Ernest Lemberger and the deputy of mission (later chargé d'affaires) Gerald Hinteregger both responded enthusiastically. But we soon ran into a serious problem. It seems that a few years before Austria had made a similar gift to Lincoln Center in New York, and Lobmeyr's three competitors—Bakalwitz Sohn, Kalmar, and Joseph Zahn—had objected vigorously and effectively, creating a minor cause célèbre. As a result, the Austrian Parliament had decided there would be no more gifts of chandeliers to any foreign country.

With the hope of finding a way around this problem, I went to Vienna. On January 4, 1968, I began a series of meetings with Austrian government officials, starting with Dr. Richard Sickinger, who was handling the Center's request; Alexander Auer, chief of the cultural section; and Karl Gruber, a former ambassador to the United States. Their initial

King Olaf V of Norway visited Washington just before the Center opened. I escorted him on a tour of the facilities and showed him his country's gift of 11 Hadelands chandeliers in the Concert Hall.

reaction was discouraging. Austria would like very much to be represented in the Kennedy Center with an exemplary gift, they told me. How about tapestries? I said no. How about iron grillwork? I said no; Lobmeyr chandeliers were what our architect wanted for the Opera House, and nothing else would do. Surely, I said, there must be a way that Austria could make such a gift without violating the will of Parliament. They said they would see what they could do.

More meetings followed. Over the next 10 days I conferred several times with Hans Rath, head of the family that owned Lobmeyr, as well as with Gruber, who was now attached to the chancellor's office. I also had fruitful conversations with Milos Franc, the former commercial counselor at the Washington embassy, and with Fritz Gleissner, the head of a delegation from the Austrian Chamber of Commerce. Gleissner was the son of an old friend of mine who had been governor of Upper Austria. As negotiations proceeded, his role proved to be pivotal.

Everyone I talked with was gracious, cooperative, and of a mind to work out a solution, but it soon became clear that any deal would have to satisfy three parties—the Austrian government, the Austrian Chamber of

Commerce, and J. & L. Lobmeyr. Tragically, our negotiations were interrupted by news of Hans Rath's sudden death in a train accident.

Rath's son Peter, then in his twenties, soon replaced him, and after a short interval negotiations were resumed, continuing in Washington and Vienna. Finally, terms were defined that all parties could agree to: Lobmeyr would design and furnish chandeliers for the Opera House with the understanding that payment would not be made by the government but by the Austrian Chamber of Commerce and its associates; Lobmeyr would, for "public service considerations," reduce the cost from $150,000 to $50,000; and the Austrian government would appropriate $40,000, all of it to go to Lobmeyr's competitors for the purchase of lighting fixtures and chandeliers. Once approved, the arrangement was officially confirmed in a letter from Ambassador Lemberger to our State Department.

As it turned out, Lobmeyr furnished the spectacular chandelier treatment for the Opera House, and the three competitors furnished chandeliers, from classic to modern design, for other important areas of the Center. Designed by Peter Rath, the Lobmeyr chandelier is truly a gem. It is 60 feet in diameter and comprises 136 crystal elements, lighted by 3,247 bulbs. Stone believed it to be worth at least $250,000.

I had been negotiating since 1964 with the Belgian ambassador Richard Scheyven and his cultural counselor, Ernest Staes, for a Belgian gift. The two-year negotiations required the utmost diplomacy and tact. Belgium first offered miniature sculptures by Mener, but although they were beautiful, the Center did not have an appropriate place to display them. Belgium also offered tapestries. We finally settled on a very fine gift for the Grand Foyer—more than 100 mirrors of 8,300 square feet, 60 feet high, valued at $50,000. The mirrors were specially crated and shipped, and Belgium sent its own experts over to install them. Many people think the Grand Foyer rivals the Hall of Mirrors at Versailles, thanks to this generous gift from Belgium.

Negotiations for a gift from Japan were initiated by me with Genichi Akatani, counselor at the Japanese embassy. We had become very close friends while reinitiating the Cherry Blossom Festival in Washington after the war. Amb. Teruo Hachia, executive director of the America-Japan Society in Tokyo, was supportive. Akatani devised the idea of a gift of a silk curtain for the Opera House. In this case the Japanese government appro-

GIFTS FROM FOREIGN COUNTRIES

AFRICA: The African Room, constructed and decorated through the generosity of nations on the continent of Africa.

ARGENTINA: A bronze sculpture by Libero Badii on the first tier of the Concert Hall; two oil paintings by Raquel Forner in the box tier of the Opera House.

AUSTRALIA: Seven tapestries representing The Creation designed by John Coburn for the South Gallery.

AUSTRIA: A Lobmeyr crystal chandelier and additional light fixtures for the Opera House.

BELGIUM: Mirrors for the Grand Foyer and Opera House.

BRAZIL: Fiberwork sculpture by Jacques Douchez in the Hall of States.

BULGARIA: A sculpture by Professor V. Minekov.

CANADA: Eisenhower Theater stage curtain.

COLOMBIA: A metal sculpture by Eduardo Ramirez on the south circular drive.

CYPRUS: An ancient amphora for the box tier of the Eisenhower Theater.

DENMARK: A porcelain relief by Inge Lise Koefoed for the Concert Hall Lobby.

EGYPT: An alabaster vase, circa 2600 B.C., for the box tier of the Eisenhower Theater.

FINLAND: Chinaware for the restaurants.

FRANCE: Two tapestries by Henri Matisse and two sculptures by Henri Laurens for the box tier of the Opera House.

GERMANY: Bronze panels sculptured by Jurgen Weber placed along the entrance plaza.

GREAT BRITAIN: Sculpture by Dame Barbara Hepworth for the box tier of the Concert Hall.

GREECE: A museum replica of the bronze statue of Poseidon for the box tier of the Opera House.

INDIA: Twenty specially designed planters for the Grand Foyer, Hall of Nations, and Hall of States.

IRAN: Two silk and wool rugs designed for the anteroom of the south lounge of the Opera House.

IRELAND: Waterford crystal chandeliers with four matching sconces for the south lounge of the Opera House.

ISRAEL: Artwork and complete furnishings for the Concert Hall lounge.

ITALY: All the marble for the exterior and interior of the building, cut to specifications.

JAPAN: The Opera House stage curtain and, as a Bicentennial gift to America, the Terrace Theater.

LUXEMBOURG: Sculpture by Lucian Wercollier for the box tier of the Concert Hall.

MALAYSIA: Shadow puppets from Ramayana epics.

MEXICO: Two tapestries by Leonardo Nierman for the box tier of the Eisenhower Theater.

MOROCCO: black-and-white wool rugs for the Roof Terrace galleries.

NETHERLANDS: A 17th-century oil painting by P.G. van Roestraeten for the south lounge of the Opera House.

NORWAY: Eleven Hadelands crystal chandeliers for the Concert Hall.

PAKISTAN: Two Bokhara rugs for the South Opera lounge.

PERU: A painting by Antonio Maro in the Hall of Nations.

PORTUGAL: Planters created from ceramic tiles designed by Mario da Silva, North and South Gallery.

SPAIN: Two tapestries reproduced from original paintings by Goya for the South Opera lounge; sculpture of Don Quixote by Aurelio Teno for the east lawn.

SRI LANKA: Two handcrafted standing brass oil lamps in the anteroom of the South Opera lounge.

SWEDEN: Eighteen Orrefors crystal chandeliers for the Grand Foyer.

SWITZERLAND: A sculpture by Willy Weber for the Concert Hall lobby.

THAILAND: Thai silk for furnishings.

TUNISIA: Reproduction of a third century mosaic for the roof terrace.

TURKEY: Porcelain vases designed by Muhsin Demironat.

YUGOSLAVIA: Tapestries by Jagoda Buic and Matega Rocci.

priated $70,000 to be matched by private contributions. The government gave the money to the America-Japan Society, which raised additional money from private sources to cover any excess amount required for the red and gold curtain, as the total cost was $150,000. The Nishijin Textile Industry Cooperative, in conjunction with the Design Department of Kyoto, fashioned this curtain from patterns of traditional Noh costumes. A jacquard loom, the largest in the world, had been specially designed for its manufacture. The presentation of the curtain, valued at $300,000, was made at the Japanese embassy on February 9, 1967. Interestingly, the presentation preceded completion of the Center by at least three years, and it was necessary to crate and store the curtain while construction progressed. The National Gallery of Art and the Smithsonian Institution both advised on the proper method of conservation. Security Storage of Washington was charged with this task, and when the curtain was opened and hung three years later, it was in perfect condition.

Amb. Gordon Hamilton Southam, director of the new cultural center in Ottawa, was primarily responsible for a gift from Canada, a curtain for the Eisenhower Theater valued at $70,000. Designed by Mme. Mariette Rousseau-Vermette, one of Canada's foremost artists, the curtain was pre-

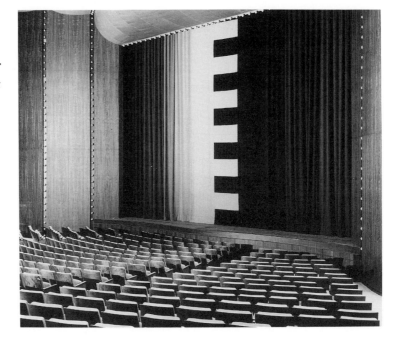

The Eisenhower Theater curtain, a gift from Canada.

The Opera House Lobmeyr crystal chandelier, a gift from Austria, is 60 feet in diameter and has 3,247 lamps.

The author, Roger Stevens, and Amb. Ernest Lemberger at presentation ceremony. On this occasion the ambassador gave the Center a sculptured crystal bowl with engravings of the Vienna Statsopera as a symbol of Austrian-American friendship.

sented in a ceremony at the Center by Susan Eisenhower, the president's granddaughter, on April 16, 1970.

Sweden's gift began with negotiations between myself and Amb. Hubert de Besche in 1965. The ambassador had proposed a gift of chandeliers for the Grand Foyer, for which the Swedish Parliament had appropriated funds. Negotiations were suddenly put on hold, however, when he received a communication from his foreign office informing him of a visit from Eugene Black of the World Bank with a letter from Jacqueline Kennedy requesting a similar gift to the Kennedy Library in Boston. Before traveling to Stockholm, I met with LeMoyne Billings, Mary Lasker, and Roger Stevens. This was a delicate situation because we did not want to offend Mrs. Kennedy. All agreed I should proceed to Sweden, and on September 2, 1966, I visited the Foreign Ministry and met with Swedish officials. I made the case for the Kennedy Center: it was located in Washington—the seat of our government, the site of diplomatic missions, and a major tourist attraction—and though Boston was a great city, it did not draw the millions of visitors the nation's capital did. Once the Foreign Ministry was convinced that the gift should go to the Center, the funds were voted and work began on the 18 magnificent handblown chandeliers designed by Orrefors. Each weighs more than a ton, requiring reenforcement of the ceiling.

During these fund-raising efforts we had not ignored foundations. In March 1963, the Ford Foundation offered the Center a generous conditional matching grant of $5 million, payable when the Center's fund-raising total reached $15 million. In October 1963, we received an unrestricted gift of $1 million from the Rockefeller Foundation.

Fund raising was a continuing effort. President Kennedy and his administration cooperated fully. Indeed, the president had grand plans for 1964, scheduling a White House affair for January, at which he expected to raise large amounts of money. Minimum contributions from those in attendance were to be $100,000! Mrs. Kennedy also did more than serve as honorary chairman. She designed and painted two beautiful Christmas cards, which Hallmark printed as a public service with all proceeds going to the Center. The company reported that it sold seven times more of these cards than of any other.

The original act in 1958 had provided a five-year period for the trustees to raise the necessary funds by voluntary contributions. By June 3, 1963, pledges and contributions had reached a little over $10 million, which included the gift of marble from the Italian government and the $5 million grant from the Ford Foundation. Expenses had been kept to a minimum. We paid salaries only to the assistant to the executive vice president and to the secretary and staff coordinator. The rest of the expenses had gone toward the closed-circuit telecast, public relations, and fund-raising efforts. Even so, it was self-evident that a September 3, 1963, statutory deadline to raise $30 million could not be met.

On August 3, 1963, only a few months before his death, President Kennedy signed legislation increasing the number of trustees and extending the time for raising private funds. At the signing ceremony were the author, Rep. Robert Jones, Rep. James Wright, James Buckley (a Center trustee), Charlotte Reid (trustee), Center Chairman Roger Stevens, and Rep. Frank Thompson.

Since early in his stewardship, Stevens had felt keenly that the board of general trustees needed to be increased from 15 to 30 to create a broader geographic base to raise funds. The board unanimously accepted this recommendation, and House and Senate trustees introduced legislation to increase the number of general trustees as requested as well as to extend for three years the time to raise funds.

In testimony to Congress, Stevens and I made the point that the change in administrations resulted in an inevitable delay in the Center's activities, which temporarily stalled the program. We emphasized, however, that progress had been made.

The debate over the extension proved gratifying. Some former opponents of the Center had changed their minds. Ranking Republican congressman James Auchincloss of New Jersey, after efforts of Janet Auchincloss, his cousin, and of Rep. Carroll Reece (R-Tenn.), his close colleague, supported the legislation, as did Reps. John C. Kunkel (R-Pa.), James Cleveland (R-N.H.), and Paul M. McCloskey (R-Calif.). The legislation passed easily, and Kennedy signed the bill on August 19, 1963.

4

DEATH OF JFK:
The Center Becomes a National Memorial

On the afternoon of Friday, November 22, 1963, I waited with the groceries in front of the store while my wife, Ann, went cheerfully to pick up the car. When she returned, I was shocked by the expression on her face. She said she'd just heard a report by Walter Cronkite that President Kennedy had been shot in Dallas. It was a five-minute drive to our home. As we entered the house, reports came over the radio that the president was dead.

Over the weeks that followed, an almost spontaneous movement arose, here and abroad, to honor the president's memory. Kennedy plazas, places, schools, boulevards, streets, and hospitals were designated all over the world. Mayor Robert Wagner of New York City changed the name of Idlewild International Airport to John F. Kennedy International Airport. The U.S. Treasury minted a Kennedy half-dollar. Queen Elizabeth of England set aside three acres at Runnymede, near Windsor Castle, where King John had signed the Magna Carta, as a Kennedy shrine. A huge John F. Kennedy memorial park was created in New Ross, southern Ireland, near his family's ancestral homestead in Dunjanstown. Canada named one of its tallest peaks Mount Kennedy. And in Boston, what would have been the Kennedy Presidential Library after his retirement became instead the John F. Kennedy Memorial Library.

Like everyone else, Ann and I mourned the nation's loss and felt the common impulse to express our grief. When, on the evening of the tragedy, she said, "Wouldn't the Center be a wonderful memorial to the president?" I said yes and immediately phoned Stevens in New York. His reaction was prompt and positive. The Center would be a fitting embodiment of Kennedy's conviction that the country was approaching its cultural majority. Furthermore, we agreed, the idea would command bipartisan support because of Kennedy's stated commitment to carry out Eisenhower's initiative. I then phoned Mary Lasker. She was equally supportive of the proposal and called LeMoyne Billings. Shortly thereafter, Lem phoned me. One of the president's closest friends, he was still in a state of shock. He said that he was staying at the White House that weekend and promised to get back to me. Sometime later he called to say that he had arranged for an appointment with President Johnson's representative at the White House for Monday, November 25, one hour after the funeral.

After discussions with Stevens and Lasker, I phoned Everett McKinley Dirksen (R-Ill.), the Senate majority leader, and Sen. Leverett Saltonstall (R-Mass.), a trustee. Over that same weekend I also spoke with Jim Wright, a member of the House Public Works Committee; Richard Sullivan, the committee's general counsel; Bob Jones, chairman of a subcommittee of the Public Works committee; and Sen. Jennings Randolph (D-W.Va.). We all were in favor of the Center as a memorial. To alert the press, I phoned George Beveridge of the *Washington Evening Star* and Richard L. Coe and Marie Smith (later Schwartz) of the *Washington Post*.

Once the White House meeting was scheduled, Lasker arranged for a small group to convene before the funeral that same day, November 25, at the home of Florence Mahoney in Georgetown. Thomas Deegan (the Center's public relations representative), Lasker, Billings, Stevens, and I discussed the proposed renaming of the Center as well as the need for funds necessary to complete the project.

Billings and I were designated to present the case, and we went to the White House together from Mrs. Mahoney's. We met in the office of Myer (Mike) Feldman, President Johnson's representative and spokesman. Also present were Larry O'Brien, Arthur Schlesinger, and Stephen Smith, President Kennedy's brother-in-law. Lem and I briefed them on the status of the National Cultural Center, especially the estimated $50 million necessary to build it. Feldman responded that "whatever the Kennedy family wished, [President Johnson] would carry out." Apparently, all we needed was an expression of assent from the Kennedys.

After the meeting, Billings went upstairs to say goodbye to the

Kennedy family. When he returned, he appeared to be uneasy. He told me then, and upon returning to Mrs. Mahoney's residence repeated to those present, that he had had "a violent conversation" with Bobby Kennedy about the proposed change of name. He said that Bobby Kennedy had told him that Bill Walton (David Finley's successor as chairman of the Commission of Fine Arts) had spoken to him about another memorial in Washington. Walton's plan was to rename Pennsylvania Avenue "Kennedy Avenue." There would be no cost to the taxpayers, and it would be fitting to have this historic half-mile route connecting the Capitol to the White House—"the President's Avenue, the Grand Avenue"—named after Kennedy.

Those present did not like Walton's idea. As someone said, it was "small potatoes" compared to a national cultural center for the performing arts, which would be a living memorial. So the decision became something of a contest between Billings and Walton, who was also highly regarded by the Kennedy family. Billings was discouraged. Although he was invited to attend the family meeting the following morning (November 26) to discuss the subject, he did not want to go. He was convinced that Walton had already won over Bobby Kennedy.

The company at the Mahoney residence persuaded Billings to attend the meeting anyway; after all, we argued, we had nothing to lose by trying. So he returned to the White House the next morning. All who had met at Mrs. Mahoney's the night before waited anxiously for word on the outcome. He called early in the afternoon to report that the family had agreed to the renaming of the Center in memory of Kennedy.

Newbold Noyes, editor of the *Evening Star*, had phoned during the meeting at Mrs. Mahoney's to say that he was writing a piece advocating that the national cultural center be named after President Kennedy. The next day the *Star* carried a front-page editorial. The *Star* had been a consistent supporter of the Center and of the river site, unlike the *Post*, whose editorials and columnists, conspicuously Wolf von Eckhardt, had often been at odds with us on issues of design and location.

Later, however, the name change brought unqualified approval even from the *Post*, and the idea began to develop real momentum. In Congress many bills were introduced to make the Center a memorial for the slain president. One of them, and the only one that truly counted, was initiated by the White House. Just as Feldman had said he would, President Johnson followed the family's wishes, and on December 3, 1963, the administration bill (Senate Joint Resolution [S.J. Res.] 136) was introduced by Senator Fulbright with bipartisan cosponsorship. Of extraordinary significance, the bill authorized the federal government to match dollar for dollar the funds raised from the private sector for the Center's construction, now budgeted at $50 million. The prospect of federal participation in the financing of the project represented a momentous change from the original concept.*

Simultaneously, companion legislation was introduced in the House (House Joint Resolution [H.J. Res.] 828) by the chairman of the Public Works Committee, Charles A. Buckley. Through the efforts of Representative Jones, counsel Sullivan, and Senator McNamara, chairman of the Senate Public Works Committee, arrangements were made for an unprecedented joint session of the House and Senate committees.

President Johnson, sensitive to the public mood, seized the opportunity to move quickly. He followed the joint bill's introduction with a letter of strong support to the chairmen of the two committees.

On December 11, the night before the scheduled hearing, Mary Lasker held a dinner at the City Tavern to discuss the proposed legislation. A realist and experienced hand on legislative matters as well as fund raising, she said there was no way the trustees could raise $25 million from the private sector to match a similar government grant. She recommended that a formula be devised to raise only $15 million in matching funds. Jones and Sullivan participated in the discussions.

After dinner, Jones, Sullivan, and I joined a staff member from the legislative drafting section. We worked in Jones's office until the early hours of the morning to prepare a revised bill. It was introduced (H.J. Res. 871) on December 13, the day after the hearing opened, and it superseded previous bills to become the amended administration bill finally enacted. The changes called for us to raise $15.5 million, to be matched by $15.5

---

* In retrospect I think it unlikely that a project as complex as the Center could ever have been finished without some significant contribution from the federal government. There were times, however, when having Congress as a fund-raising partner struck me as a peculiarly mixed blessing. Dealing with Capitol Hill is not the happiest of occupations, and the requisite procedures for record-keeping and accounting demanded not only patience and a scrupulous attention to detail but sometimes a kind of creative improvisation more natural to a good actor than to a lawyer like myself.

million in government funds. An additional $15.4 million, earmarked for the underground parking facility, would be raised by borrowing from the U.S. Treasury, a device for which the precedent had been established by the St. Lawrence Seaway Authority. As evidence of the loan, the Treasury would issue revenue bonds to the Center—in effect, IOUs—providing for graduated rates of interest. The bill further provided (1) that the Center be the sole national memorial to the late John Fitzgerald Kennedy within the city of Washington and its environs, and (2) that an appropriate tribute to his memory be created, with approval of the Smithsonian Institution, within the building.

DESPITE THE OUTPOURING of public sentiment, our bill met some painful opposition at the hearing.* Rep. William B. Widnall (R-N.J.), a tenacious adversary, wanted to delay consideration altogether and proposed instead the creation of a Kennedy memorial commission. He quoted at length from architectural critic Wolf von Eckhardt and referred to Patrick Hayes's objections to the Center's location and design. He spoke vehemently against the proposal for a bond obligation—what he called "a first mortgage"—on a presidential memorial, contending that it would be the first one in history. And he observed that, in the past, Center officials had estimated the cost of the superstructure but not that of the substructure. Stevens and others, he implied, were misleading Congress by not disclosing that the fund-raising goal of $31 million excluded the cost of parking facilities. Plainly, he did not know about "the Lasker meeting" of the day before.

Republican congressman William Cramer of Florida, interrogating

---

* From inception through construction, opposition to the Center was always with us, but it was not always easy to gauge or understand. I am sure that some of the opposition was ideologically grounded, for there were many conservatives in Congress who believed devoutly that no government had any business in the arts, especially the performing arts, and there were others who thought with equal sincerity that government support might be proper but only at the state and local levels. As the project went along, the focus of the controversy shifted, and quite constructive debates ensued over issues of location, design, and purpose. There were times, however, when the attacks on the Center were undoubtedly nothing more than the flexing of partisan politics, and I must say that some of our critics were less than gentlemanly, as when they accused the trustees of "boondoggling" and likened Stone's design to a "box of Kleenex." Outside the government, many of our critics were clearly, however irrationally, stirred by the smell of profit, especially when the time came for us to square the site by buying up private lands.

Trustees Edward Kennedy and Mary Lasker.

us at length, questioned the use of pledges instead of cash for matching fund purposes and then zeroed in on the financing of the parking garage. He said he was stunned by our failure to disclose, in previous public appeals for contributions, the approximately $11 million needed for construction of the parking facility.

Stevens responded that we did not plan to seek public contributions for parking facilities because we did not see "how in fairness to the people in other parts of the country it would be a logical part of the National Cultural Center." And as for the question, which repeatedly arose, over Congress's failure to use a commission to study the memorial before moving so quickly to rename the Center, Jones reminded the committee that the Robert A. Taft Memorial on Capitol Hill had been approved by Congress without going through a commission study. As he said, "It was received on the floor on July 22, 1955, and the House passed it on July 25."

Fortunately, the Center had a score of able defenders, perhaps none more committed or influential than Bob Jones. Also of inestimable value was the support of House Public Works Committee chairman Buckley. A modest man but a skilled politician, Buckley had an excellent eye for talent. One of his protégés was Sullivan, whose skills and wisdom I now came to appreciate even more.

Listening to the testimony, I was struck by the eloquence that the prospect of the National Cultural Center inspired in its proponents. Architect Edward Durell Stone was especially moving when he spoke of what the Center could mean for the nation and our time:

> You realize, in historically great periods when art flourished, there was peace, stable government, and prosperity. We've had good fortune to enjoy this climate. It remained, however, for President and Mrs. Eisenhower and for President and Mrs. Kennedy to provide the inspiration and leadership. This they did in full measure so that we are, in reality, in the beginning of a great Renaissance in the intellectual and artistic life of this country. As a creative artist, I find consolation in the statement that all great periods in history were only great because of the art they produced.

Stevens and I did not reach such levels of rhetoric at the December 12 hearing. We did, however, answer some tough questions about the original administration bill.

Members of Congress were getting increasingly testy with the approach of the Christmas recess and impatient with anything that threatened a delay. Our hope, of course, was for passage before the recess, and the chances looked good. On Friday, December 13, the amended administration bill was introduced by Buckley and made part of the record before its second-day hearing on the 16th.

Unfortunately, the first witness was New Jersey congressman Widnall. He again raised many questions, many a rehash of his previous arguments. He refocused on the surprise testimony that the $31 million requested for the Center did not include the cost of the parking facility. He also criticized the haste with which the legislation had been prepared; in truth, we had come up with a new bill less than 24 hours after the interrogation by Representative Cramer. Bluntly, Widnall wanted to know: "Is the memorial concept a 'face-saver' for an otherwise faltering project?" He again challenged the idea that the concept would fit into such a small parcel of acreage and complained of putting a first mortgage on a presidential memorial.

Outstanding witnesses, however, defended the plan, probably the most important of whom was Dr. Leonard Carmichael, secretary of the Smithsonian. Carmichael, an ex officio member of the Center's board of trustees, said:

The matter under consideration is of high importance for the welfare of all the performing arts in our nation. When the Center is complete, it will provide a brilliant and appropriate showcase in which America and the rest of the world can properly admire our country's aesthetic achievements in the arts that are recognized as a basic in every civilization that can be called great.

Other public officials well regarded in Congress also lent their support. Responding to the concern about the size of the site, T. Sutton Jett, regional director of the NPS, made it clear that since the inception of the Center, the Park Service

[o]ffered to accommodate the adjoining park development to enhance the beauty of the Center. . . . As the concept of the building developed, the limitations of the site became apparent. We have assisted the architects in developing site plans. . . . The Department of Interior is eager to continue its cooperation with the board of trustees and the National Capital Planning Commission in every way possible to assure that an adequate site as well as parklands involved will be available to bring to fruition this most worthy undertaking.

Similarly, Secretary of Interior Udall made it clear that his department had the "responsibility for administering much of the land that is necessary if the Center is to become a reality." His department, he said, would cooperate in every way to make available all the land necessary. Udall, a friend of President Kennedy, moved from prosaic to poetic in completing his remarks when he referred to President Kennedy's statement on receiving an honorary degree at Amherst College a month before his assassination. That statement is now carved in marble on the exterior wall of the Kennedy Center:

I look forward to an America which will reward achievement in the arts as we reward achievement in business or statecraft. I look forward to an America which will steadily raise the standards of artistic accomplishment and which will steadily enlarge cultural opportunities for all of our citizens. And I look forward to an America which commands respect throughout the world not only for its strength but for its civilization as well.

The Public Works Committee approved the bill in a report dated December 17, 1963. Filled with sentiments about President Kennedy and the best that America has to offer, one part of the report nevertheless gave the board of trustees concern.

> Pledges are not to be considered as having been received or held by the Board for purposes of matching by Federal government until such time as those pledges are reduced to money or other assets actually held by the Board.

Also, the report gave no credit for more than $1 million that already was received and expended for the benefit of construction. Otherwise, though, it approved Buckley's administration bill, providing for $15.5 million in appropriations to match private contributions on a dollar-for-dollar basis and authorizing us to borrow $15.4 million from the U.S. Treasury for construction of the parking facility.

The following day, December 18, Chairman Buckley requested a rule from the Rules Committee (which is necessary before any bill can go to the floor of the full House). Unexpectedly, there was opposition to the appropriation of federal dollars on a matching basis, resulting in a compromise that, in effect, would bring the legislation to a vote in the House in January after the Christmas recess.

Meanwhile, the Senate Public Works Committee had approved the bill the previous day. Senator McNamara's report was similar to the report of the House Public Works Committee. One reference, however, is worth quoting:

> It should be noted that when George Washington, in 1789, commissioned Pierre L'Enfant to plan a Federal City, he directed that it be planned as a cultural and civic center for the United States. Completion of this cultural center will carry out the wishes of our first President as well as those of our late President Kennedy and fulfill the hopes of the Nation that have been frustrated for so many years.

On December 18, 1963, Senate Majority Leader Michael Mansfield (D-Mont.), a powerful Center advocate, requested unanimous consent to consider S.J. Res. 136, which included the amended version of the bill introduced by Representative Buckley in the House. Senator McNamara, on behalf of the Senate Committee and the 51 Senate sponsors of this joint resolution, urged favorable consideration. No amendment was proposed and the bill passed unanimously by a voice vote.

The Buckley bill was brought up in the House on January 8, 1964. Adversaries introduced amendments in an attempt to kill the bill, or at least delay it. All such efforts were overwhelmingly defeated, but not before opponents made some telling criticisms.

H. R. Gross of Iowa, for example, the self-appointed fiscal watchdog of the Congress, questioned the appropriations. Attacking the legislation by referring to President Johnson's hopes for the poor, he said:

> Mr. Speaker, in view of the so-called State of the Union message that we heard only a few minutes ago and the time spent by President Johnson telling us of the poverty-stricken in this country, as well as [of] the spending the federal government must do to take care of the multitude of impoverished, I think it is most audacious on the part of the Democratic leadership of the House of Representatives to call up the cultural center bill this afternoon.

Other critics went even further. While Rep. Clarence Brown (R-Ohio) agreed with the laudatory comments his colleagues made about the late President Kennedy, he opposed the legislation on economic grounds. He commented:

> I have a feeling deep down in my bones, as we say in southern Ohio, that perhaps some people here in Washington saw in that tragic happening the opportunity to unload the project that they had failed to put over in the form of this cultural center by suggesting that it be renamed the John F. Kennedy Center as a tribute to the late, lamented president to be operated under a board of trustees.

For the first time in history, he said, the U.S. government is putting up $15.5 million in "hard cash" and a borrowing authority from the federal Treasury of $15.4 million to build

> a three-level garage underneath the Cultural Center. This garage is

to be near the Potomac, where they probably will have to pump the Potomac River out of it every few days. If the garage does not pay off—and I don't believe there is anyone in the world that will tell you it will pay off—the federal Treasury is to pick up the tab. How? By a back-door approach?

His prediction about the Treasury bonds should not go unnoticed. The Center did indeed find it impossible to pay the interest on the bonds, and in 1984 legislation was approved canceling accumulated interest of

In January 1964, President Lyndon B. Johnson signed a bill to convert the Center into a living memorial to John F. Kennedy. The month before, congressional leaders took a break from hearings of the Senate and House Public Works committees to inspect Stone's model. From left: Rep. Harold Ryan, Rep. Robert Jones, Sen. Jennings Randolph, Sen. Hiram Fong, Rep. Charles Buckley, Sen. J. William Fulbright (a Center trustee), and Sen. Leverett Saltonstall (trustee).

more than $30 million. The new arrangement had an unusual provision: under it, principal would be repaid over a period of 20 years; against these payments would be credited interest accrued on payments to principal previously made.

On January 10, 1964, the bill passed the House by a voice vote. On January 23, President Johnson used 34 pens to sign it into law (P.L. 88-620). In approving the bill, Johnson spoke of Kennedy's active concern with the progress of the Center and of his hope that he might see it completed during his term of office:

> It is, therefore, I think, entirely fitting that the Center should be named in his memory and should be dedicated anew to the great purposes for which it was originally concerned. By this bill, federal funds are provided to match money donated by private sources. The Center will become a fine example of cooperation between citizens and their government. . . .
>
> The Kennedy Center for the Performing Arts is not simply a Washington building. It is a national institution. The vitality and the well-being of the people are closely related to their capacity to always produce a high level of art, and to enjoy it and to appreciate it.
>
> In signing this act, I am aware of its far-ranging consequences. I am confident that we have chosen well that the institution now given the breath of life will have a long and distinguished future. All those who worked in this cause can now know that they are not only honoring the memory of a very great man, but they are enriching our whole American life.

One hurdle had been crossed, but there was a hard course ahead. We still had to raise the money, assemble the land, and supervise construction. None of these tasks proved to be easy.

5

PROGRESS:
We Break Ground but Our Critics Won't Quit

*E*uphoria over Congress's action did not last long. The act to rename the Center had authorized matching funds, but the money would be forthcoming only when Congress followed through with an appropriation. That required another round of legislation.

President Johnson submitted our appropriations bill on February 14, 1964, requesting $15.5 million to the Center (provided we raised a like amount in private funds) and an additional $3.3 million to the NCPC to be used for the Center's benefit. To our immense gratification, the president's requests went to Congress with approval of the Bureau of the Budget, which by law was responsible for evaluating the fiscal impact of all legislation.*

On February 20 and 24, 1964, hearings were held before the House Subcommittee on Appropriations to consider the Department of Interior and related agency appropriations for 1965. That year's appropriations bill for the Department of Interior and related agencies was slightly over $1.9 billion. Yet in the two days of hearings, more testimony was presented on the $18.8 million for the Center than on all the other items combined.

Not unexpectedly, introduction of our appropriations bill triggered renewed attacks from our critics, all of them voicing variations on a familiar theme—that our proposal to rename the Center was a desperate

---

* Our relations with the bureau were always cordial. In the genesis of the Center, three bureau directors—Percival Brundage, Maurice Stans, and Elmer Staats—were particularly helpful, as were Phillip S. Hughes, director of legislation, and two of his assistants, Wilfred Rommell and Joe English.

act to save a misconceived project. Once again, Roger Stevens and I were called to testify at congressional hearings.

During the hearings, Representative Widnall asked written questions, to which pro-Center congressmen expected Stevens and me to reply. Widnall and his allies did not have the votes to block the legislation, but they were determined to use every strategy in the book to delay it. Adversaries outside Congress were also vocal. They got media coverage, which unfortunately created an impression that the Center was "pie in the sky" and would never become a reality. We were made aware that opposition of a like nature had left unfunded a memorial to Franklin D. Roosevelt despite approval of a commission in 1955.

During the hearings, members supporting the Center introduced lengthy testimony. When our turn came, Stevens and I reviewed the highlights of the Kennedy Center Act. We covered thoroughly the concept of the Center; the fund-raising program and plans for the future; the designs of Edward Durell Stone; and the use of GSA as agent for design work and construction. We reported on our plans for the underground parking facility, the condition of the soil, the prospect of flooding, and procedures for land acquisition. We went into virtually every aspect of financing, accounting, and administration.

While obviously supporting the proposed appropriation of $15.5 million in government funds to match private donations, we emphasized what to our minds was the key provision: the additional $3.3 million necessary for the NCPC to acquire land not only within but also outside the statutory-designated site. This land was necessary to meet the requirements of Stone's design. It would provide adequate access to and from the Center's 1,600-car parking facility and would ensure that the Center be in a parklike setting.

Legal issues were raised for several years over the acquisition of this additional land, and they were always rebutted vigorously by Daniel Shear, NCPC counsel. His opinion was based on Section 2 of the act of June 6, 1924, which gave the commission authority to acquire lands for park and parkway purposes. Shear and other members of the NCPC staff, along with the commissioners themselves, were unfailingly cooperative, particularly when it came to problems of site development, ingress, egress, and traffic flow. The same was true of the NPS and officials of the District of Columbia, as well as of the D.C. Highway Department under Tom Arris.

The original Potomac River site contained approximately 7.5 acres, 1.8 acres of which had been privately owned in 1958 and were being gradually acquired by the NCPC for our purposes. (Agencies of the U.S. government, chiefly the NPS, owned the rest.) Of the $3.3 million that the appropriations bill earmarked for the NCPC, $2 million was for acquisition of the remaining privately owned lands. About $500,000 was for the purchase of two needed parcels outside the site, one of which was a tract occupied by the Watergate Inn. The remaining $800,000 was to replace an equal amount that the NCPC had used earlier to acquire land for the Center. This last sum had been drawn from sums appropriated for the park, parkway, and playground system of the District of Columbia under Section 4 of the act of May 29, 1930, as amended, commonly known as the Capper-Crampton Act (46 Stat. 842). With approval of the D.C. commissioners, Capper-Crampton funds had been used on behalf of the Center to the point that no more money was available for the completion of other projects; unless the funds were restored, the District's children would be denied a number of promised playgrounds.

Through condemnation proceedings, NCPC had acquired the Bluebell Waffle and Donut Shop for $86,000. It also acquired a small but critical piece of land adjoining the site, thanks to the generosity of L. Corrin Strong, who provided a deed of gift to the United States in the amount of $57,000. A few congressmen "nitpicked" about how we were carrying this gift on the books, but without it NCPC would have been unable to make the necessary acquisition. That is how critical our funding problems had become.

Questions about land took much of the congressional committee's time as critics tried to undermine the site's feasibility for a building of the Center's design and purpose. The questions continued despite testimony from the NPS that the location had been recommended by a task force under Conrad L. Wirth which, along with the Corps of Engineers, had been studying all possibilities for more than four years, almost from the day Stone presented his first concept. Robert C. Horne, deputy regional director for the NPS, addressed our critics forthrightly:

> Washington is known as a city in the park. The Capitol, the
> Mall, the Jefferson Memorial, and the Lincoln Memorial are among

those in renowned settings. Facing upon the Potomac River across the Rock Creek and Potomac Parkway with parklands extending southward to the Lincoln Memorial and beyond provides an incomparable setting. The east is open space and the north [is] open space interrupted by private property in Square 10. It is inconsistent that the Center should have so closely adjacent any background whatsoever that would so adversely influence this park setting. The cultural influence [and] the moral character of this Center dictate a requirement for the best in environmental setting, site, design, and architectural concept. The design of the Center demands open space to the north. The National Park Service therefore endorses the position of the National Capital Planning Commission and the Center to provide this unique setting for the John F. Kennedy Center for the Performing Arts. Site studies by Edward D. Stone, architect for the Center, have been developed in cooperation with the National Park Service to provide this outstanding location by accommodating the adjoining park development to enhance the beauty of this Center. Moreover, the studies indicate the necessity for relocating the roadway in the Parkway and a provision of adequate vehicular access and egress over properties now in private ownership in Square 10 adjacent to the Center. Several parcels of park, totaling about 2.3 acres of land, and a small part of Rock Creek and Potomac Parkway will be occupied by the newly designed building and its riverwood, cantilevered promenade. Additional areas proposed to be acquired with the requested appropriation and other lands in public ownership will be transferred to this department and will be made available for use of the Center and development of the site. We will continue to cooperate with the Center's board of trustees and the National Capital Planning Commission in every way possible to assist in providing an incomparable site.

In my testimony, I pointed out that the board of trustees was "carrying out the mandate of Congress" and referred to a site plan presented on January 13, 1964. A task force, consisting of officials of the District of Columbia, the NPS, the Highway Department, and the Center's engineers, was working on ingress and egress because "traffic was of vital importance."

It came as no surprise to find John Immer, president of the D.C. Federation of Citizens' Associations, among those testifying against us. By this time, too, we were prepared to hear contentious remarks from Adm. Neill Phillips, chairman of the Committee of 100 on the Federal City; only a month before, his group had passed a resolution objecting to both the river site and use of the $3.3 million for land acquisition. George Frain, the bright and hard-working legislative assistant to Rep. Frank Thompson, was an even more formidable opponent. Although always declaredly in favor of a cultural center, Frain fought the river site to the bitter end. After leaving Thompson's staff he went to work for Widnall and continued to feed ammunition to our enemies, on and off the Hill, even after the site was approved by Congress.

Despite all the fuss, in its report on March 13, 1964, the Committee on Appropriations supported the Center:

> The committee recommended the full 1964 supplemental budget request of $15.5 million representing the federal contribution to the construction of the John F. Kennedy Center for the Performing Arts as authorized by Public Law 88-620, approved January 23, 1964. This amount will become available under the terms of the Act only when and to the extent that cash contributions are available from the public to match the federal funds.
>
> Public Law 88-620 also authorized the Board of Trustees to issue Revenue Bonds through the Secretary of Treasury payable for revenues accruing to the board not to exceed $15.4 million to finance necessary parking facilities for the Center. The committee has also allowed, under the National Capital Planning Commission, the full budget request of $2.5 million to complete the acquisition of the site for the Center and to acquire essential adjacent properties to provide an appropriate parklike setting as well as exit roads for the parking garage. The committee expects that any additional funds that might be required to complete the land acquisition program will be expended from donated funds.

Debates in the House on appropriations for the Department of Interior and related agencies took place on March 17, 1964. Opponents again had their say, almost invariably following their objections to the site with requests for alternative locations. "Fiscal conservatives" such as

H. R. Gross, however, opposed the whole ball of wax: the concept of a center, the memorial to Kennedy, and the site.

Joining Gross in the attack, Rep. John Kyle (R-Iowa) brought up the purchase of the Watergate Inn. He wanted to know why the NCPC was offering only $500,000 for the Inn when a purchaser was available who would pay $900,000. He was referring to what we on the board believed to be simply another delaying ploy. A newly formed syndicate was reported to have contracted to pay $900,000 for the Inn, presumably with plans to use the site for an office complex. That was almost twice the appraised value, and I was not alone in thinking that the speculators' real intent was either to keep us from acquiring the property or to somehow make a lot of money if we did.

Challenges of this sort did not carry the day, however. In a voice vote, the House overwhelmingly supported the full appropriation.

A Senate hearing was held on March 30 with Sen. Alan Bible (D-Nev.), a strong Center advocate, presiding. Sen. Carl T. Hayden (D-Ariz.), chairman of the Committee on Appropriations, followed with his report on April 4. The committee increased the total amount for Interior, a change that required the bill to be sent to conference. On June 24, Rep. Michael J. Kirwan, an old friend of Roger Stevens, reported for the Conference Committee, which accepted the Senate version of the bill and recommended, in addition, that $225,000 be appropriated to help relocate tenants who lose their residences. A few days later, the House and Senate voted favorably to provide $18.225 million for the Kennedy Center and the NCPC. President Johnson signed the bill on July 7 (P.L. 88-356, 78 Stat. 273).*

THIS SUCCESS gave us a real boost, spurring us to proceed aggressively with fund raising, site development, and architectural plans. Stevens began a press campaign to build popular support, making much of expert engineering reports on the suitability of the site. Stone released reports aimed at relieving expressed anxieties about flooding and geological footings. Experts reported on flood control measures and soil conditions, effectively disproving the contention that the site was "a filled-in dump" and that the

---

* The authority to borrow $15.4 million from the U.S. Treasury was included in the original authorizing legislation.

building might fall into the river. Meuser, Rutledge, Wentworth, and Johnston, consulting engineers, found that the site was suitable to support the structure and, further, that it was not landfill but bedrock. When excavation started in 1965, a rock-blasting contract was among the first awarded. The Center was constructed on caissons imbedded in bedrock.

Stone also released reports on noise control techniques prepared by Dr. Cyril M. Harris, an acoustics expert retained early in the planning process on the wise advice of Lincoln Center architects. The reports outlined seven ways for controlling noise levels, most of which were later adopted.

During and after the appropriations debate, we continued to lobby locally—that is, outside Congress. We were in regular contact with the D.C. commissioners, the D.C. Zoning Commission, and other local authorities. I worked closely with the officers of the Board of Trade and its members. Bill Press rebuffed suggestions that the board renounce its support of the Potomac site; to their credit, the board's officers and directors remained firmly behind the initial 1958 resolution, and I will be forever grateful for their support of my views. One of these supporters was John Thompson, vice president of the *Washington Evening Star*, who invited me to the paper's closed family luncheons. This gave me a regular opportunity to discuss our problems.

Of all the agencies we worked with, none was more important than the NCPC. But there were vocal opponents in the NCPC as well, and Walter Louchheim was their leader. He came from the Georgetown area, was a spokesman for the Committee of 100, and indicated to Center officials that "he could very well upset the apple cart." At our request, President Johnson phoned him to talk him out of his opposition, but Louchheim was unmoved. He said he didn't care if it was the president, he would speak his own mind, and he continued to oppose everything to do with the Center. Two other members—C. McKim Norton and Dean A. M. Woodruff—followed his lead. Fortunately, on the commission were seven agencies and two congressional members (Alan Bible of the Senate and John L. McMillan of the House), as well as five citizen members appointed by the president. The chairman, Libby (Mrs. James) Rowe, represented the majority. She was a strong chairman, firm in her official decisions, and

she always supported the Center. At all meetings, however, Center supporters expected trouble from Louchheim.

Opposition in May 1964 led the NCPC the following month to

> [reaffirm] its approval of the Potomac River site and [request that]
> the chairman and staff work with the trustees of the Center and its
> staff to reconcile questions raised regarding the design of the Center
> prior to submission of the location, height, bulk, number of floors,
> size, and provision for open space in and around the Center for the
> approval by the commission in accordance with Section 16 of the Act
> of June 20, 1938 (52 Stat. 802).

This action helped the cause tremendously because it authorized
the chairman and the staff to work with the trustees of the Center on many
diverse problems, thereby facilitating accommodation of the architect's
design with reports of the task forces of the NPS, NCPC, and the District of
Columbia.

On June 4, the commission approved preliminary plans for the
Center. It took final action on July 23:

> UPON MOTION by Mr. Thiry, on behalf of the Federal Plan-
> ning and Projects Committee, seconded by Mr. Horne, and carried
> (Messrs. Louchheim and Woodruff not voting), the Commission
> approved, pursuant to Section 16 of the Act of June 20, 1938 (52 Stat.
> 802), the location, height, bulk, number of stories, and size and the
> provision for open space in and around the John F. Kennedy Center
> for the Performing Arts.

To our good fortune, this action by the NCPC confirmed that the Center
site was federal land, outside the regulations and jurisdiction of the D.C.
Zoning Commission. Otherwise, the Center would, at best, have met with
procedural delays from that commission and from the Board of Adjustment of Zoning Appeals. In truth, the action spared us what could have
been a bruising confrontation. Construction of the large Watergate complex was under way at the time, proceeding in stages under Title 75 of the
Zoning Act. The South building posed almost insoluble problems of ingress
and egress to the Center, and Center officials were on record as being

strongly opposed to its going up as planned. Regrettably, the Zoning Commission was on the side of the Watergate developers.

For some time Roger Stevens had been eager to show the public evidence of progress. He had in mind a series of events, beginning with a ground-breaking ceremony. This he staged successfully on December 2, 1964, on park property, where President Johnson appeared with the same gold-plated spade used to break ground for the Lincoln and Jefferson memorials. Johnson's remarks served both to establish the Center's significance as a national monument and to pay tribute to President Kennedy:

> This Center will be, at once, a symbol and a reflection and a hope. It will symbolize our belief that the world of creation and thought are at the core of all civilization. . . .

> Pericles said, "If Athens shall appear great to you, consider then that her glories were purchased by valiant men and by men who learned their duty." As the Center comes to reflect and advance the greatness of America, consider then those glories were purchased by a valiant leader who never swerved from duty—John Kennedy. And in his name, I dedicate this site.

As another way of demonstrating that the Center was in business, Stevens announced that it would cosponsor a national university theater festival to be held during a three-week period in the spring of 1965. The two other sponsors were the American Education Theatre Association and the American National Theatre and Academy. C. Robert Kase of the University of Delaware, a former president of ANTA, was national coordinator, appointed by the presidents of AETA and ANTA. The intent was to select about a dozen college groups to present their outstanding productions before capital audiences. For the first four years, however, only regional competitions were held. The first complete festival—four regional festivals followed by showcase presentations in Washington—was not held until 1968-69. Since then, as the American College Theater Festival, the annual event has continued without interruption, attracting participation from more than 600 colleges and universities. Just as Stevens hoped, it has made the Center a presence on community stages all across the country.

With the pending availability of government money, Center officials

President Johnson broke ground for the Center on a cold and windy morning in December 1964. The same gold-plated shovel had been used in 1914 by President Taft at the ground-breaking ceremony for the Lincoln Memorial, and in 1938 by President Franklin D. Roosevelt at a similar rite to mark the beginning of construction of the Jefferson Memorial.

'There is a quality in art which speaks across the gulf dividing man from man and nation from nation, and century from century. That quality confirms the faith that our common hopes may be more enduring than our conflicting hostilities. Even now men of affairs are struggling to catch up with the insights of great art. The stakes may well be the survival of civilizations . . .

". . . . This center will have a unique opportunity to bring together worlds of poetry and power—and bring it to the benefit of each of us. It must give special attention to the young; to increasing their interest and stimulating their creativity. It can serve as a model and instructor to other cultural centers around our Nation. It should open up new opportunities to be heard to young singers and filmmakers and playwrights. It must take the lead in bringing the best in the performing arts to every part of our beloved and rich country; so that theater and opera are not the privilege of the lucky citizens of just a few metropolitan centers.

"Yes, this is our ambitious program. But so was the vision of the man in whose memory this center is today named."

—Remarks, President Lyndon B. Johnson, ground-breaking ceremony, John F. Kennedy Center for the Performing Arts, December 2, 1964.

82

increased consultations with the offices of the secretary of Treasury and the comptroller general, the Bureau of the Budget, the Smithsonian Institution, the D.C. commissioners, and NCPC. We also improved the workings of our offices. At the annual meeting of the trustees on January 1, 1964, Philip J. Mullin was appointed administrative officer, effective in April, having been proposed by Smithsonian secretary Leonard Carmichael. During the Eisenhower years he had been assistant to Fred Seaton, secretary of Interior. Responsible for administrative and fiscal management, he served with dedication and competence throughout this tumultuous period, dealing with many vexing problems. He resigned in 1971 after the building was completed.

Another important decision in 1964 was the appointment of a memorial committee under the chairmanship of K. LeMoyne Billings. Members of this committee included Senators Fulbright and Saltonstall, Rep. Torbert H. MacDonald (D-Mass.), Jean Kennedy (Mrs. Stephen) Smith, Mary Lasker, Edward Durell Stone, S. Dillon Ripley, Theodore C. Sorensen, and Roger L. Stevens (ex officio). The committee invited, assembled, and reviewed proposals for a suitable memorial to President Kennedy to be placed within the Center building.

At about the same time, the trustees formed the Fine Arts Accessions Committee to deal with the increasing number of art objects being offered the Center. That committee was to determine acceptance or refusal of such gifts since problems with acceptance did occasionally arise and had to be handled diplomatically. Members of the Accessions Committee included Ripley, Lasker, Fulbright, and Catherine Filene (Mrs. Jouett) Shouse.

As a founding trustee of the Kennedy Center appointed by President Eisenhower in 1958, Mrs. Shouse served on the Building Committee and made a substantial financial contribution. Through the Filene Foundation, she provided a magnificent organ for the Concert Hall, and she also commissioned an organ composition by John LaMontagne. Mrs. Shouse gave continued and dedicated service until her appointment as honorary trustee. She is best known today as founder of Wolf Trap Farm Park for the Performing Arts in Vienna, Va. I served as her counsel, and as founding director and counsel for Wolf Trap. In 1977 President Ford presented her with our country's highest civilian award, the Medal of Freedom. Recently,

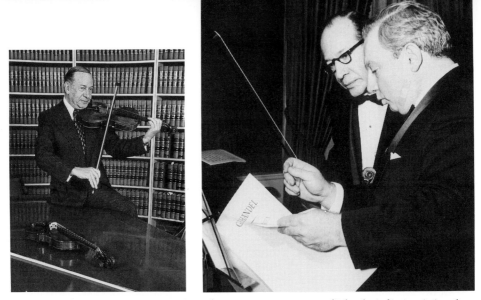

Associate Supreme Court Justice Abe Fortas, an accomplished violinist, joined us on the board in 1964. With him is Isaac Stern.

she was honored by the YWCA as one of the outstanding women of the year "for her dedication and commitment to the performing arts and for her sharing of this devotion with the American people."

The year 1964 was notable for Stevens personally, as tribute was paid to him for his contributions in the field of theater and the arts. His growing public recognition gave the Center further credibility.

Abe Fortas, a confidant of President Johnson, was appointed associate justice of the Supreme Court, as well as a trustee of the Center, in 1964. He was a close friend of and adviser to Stevens. Fortas and Mary Lasker recommended to President and Lady Bird Johnson that Stevens be appointed special assistant to the president on the arts. Stevens was so appointed on May 13, 1964, and a year later he was also named chairman of the National Council on the Arts, a position that required Senate confirmation. Republican congressman Albert H. Quie of Minnesota raised the objection of a conflict of interest as Stevens also served on the Metropolitan Opera Board and the Kennedy Center Board. I visited Quie to see if there was any way to resolve the problem. It was decided that, as NCA chairman, Stevens would make no grants to either organization.

Stevens served NCA in a superb manner in that capacity until 1970, but he nevertheless kept his focus on the Center and on the need to move forward. During continued controversy over the site and unwarranted criticism of the design of the building, he emphasized time and time again,

"Let's dig a hole in the ground and as soon as it's done, it will stop all this acrimony and opposition." He thought the ground-breaking ceremony would put a brake on the opposition. But while a ground breaking showed bona fide intentions, the site controversy continued on through 1965, when our foes made their last hopeless but troubling stand.

6

"C-DAY":
We Make the Deadline for Matching Funds

*T*he year 1965 was critical. The prospect of federal dollars was a real boost. On the other hand, the legislatively mandated deadline to raise $15.5 million in matching funds presented us with an almost overwhelming challenge. That deadline was June 30, 1965, a mere 18 months after the act's passage. It was a struggle to the last hour.

Our due date became C-Day—"Cash Day." We not only had to raise money; somehow we also had to convert pledges and gifts-in-kind into cash assets. Hearings before the Appropriations committees had made this very clear. The Center was obliged to

> match [federal funds] on a dollar-for-dollar basis. . . . Pledges are not to be considered as having been received or held by the board for the purposes of matching by the federal government until such time as those pledges are reduced to money or other assets actually held by the board.

So no money pledged, or any kind of pledged property, could be used for matching purposes. Congress's rationale was that pledges, being charitable contributions, did not always have the legal status of enforceable contracts; the law varied from state to state. What *was* certain, as anybody who has ever tried to raise money knows, was that some pledges, even though made with the best intentions, would never be collected. To count toward our goal, then, pledged property would have to be first converted into "money or other assets" actually on the Center's books.

But as I read the law, Congress was imposing no limitation on the *nature* of property that could be valued for matching purposes. To confirm my interpretation, I wrote a memorandum to the secretary of Treasury and to GAO, citing the legislative history and case law that I considered to be evidence of congressional intent. Most important, I wanted to establish as a premise for the Center's fund-raising campaign that Section 5 of the act covered *all types of property*—not merely gifts, bequests, or devises of money or securities. The act, I argued, permitted the board to receive or hold any kind of property, real or personal.

The counsel for the comptroller general (the head of GAO) and other GAO officials accepted my interpretation in principle. They nevertheless insisted that, in the conversion of pledged property into assets, every case would have to be considered on its own merits, requiring GAO review of each matching gift. This led to more meetings and, in time, to a cordial working relationship. The comptroller general, Joseph Campbell, authorized the cooperation of general counsel Frank Kelleher, a competent and dedicated civil servant. GAO assigned John Moore and his associate, Powell Marshall, both able lawyers. Also significant figures in our deliberations were Fred Smith, assistant general counsel at Treasury; Jim Bradley of the Smithsonian Institution; William A. Schmidt of GSA; and Phillip S. Hughes of the Bureau of the Budget. I came to admire and appreciate all these men, not merely for their experience and wisdom but also for their readiness to be helpful. Without any one of them, the Center would have faced perhaps insurmountable obstacles.

Early in 1965 the Center began to deal with the matter of gifts, many of which, as described in chapter 3, were from foreign governments. Most of these were still in the form of pledges, and by March it became imperative that we convert them into assets.

The comptroller general was to rule on whether the Center had the assets or property necessary to meet the congressional deadline. Treasury and GAO were cooperative and considerate, but we knew we had to deliver. To help accelerate the conversion of pledges, I turned to legal experts, as I was accustomed to doing whenever I needed help in some specialized field of law. In this instance I engaged two American University law professors, both specialists in negotiable instruments and government contracts: Robert Goostree, the acting dean, and Harold Petrowitz. Also providing

Mrs. Shouse's gift of the Concert Hall organ was valued at $112,000, but getting it credited for matching federal dollars took a bit of ingenuity.

counsel was Prof. Herbert L. Denenberg of the Wharton School of Finance, then one of the country's leading insurance authorities.

The job of converting Mrs. Shouse's gift, the organ for the Concert Hall, proved to be especially instructive. The basic contract for delivery of the organ was not between Mrs. Shouse and the Center but between the Filene Foundation, of which she was the beneficiary, and the Aeolian-Skinner Company. Since the Center was not a party to this contract, Mrs. Shouse's pledge could not be counted as an asset. Thus, I had to negotiate a change in the contract that would enable the Filene Foundation, while retaining all obligations, to assign to us its right of enforcement. Such an assignment was satisfactorily executed, in effect making the Center a third-party beneficiary.

The price of the organ to the Filene Foundation was $112,000, but before we could put this amount on our books I had to effect another change. The original contract contained a paragraph providing that the law of Massachusetts should prevail, and Massachusetts is one of the few jurisdictions in the country that does not recognize any rights of third-party beneficiaries. Since the place of performance, the District of Columbia, *does* recognize third-party rights, Aeolian-Skinner and the Filene Foundation agreed to change the jurisdiction to the District.

This arrangement was submitted to GAO and Treasury with a memorandum of law. They accepted it under a well-known principle established in *Lawrence vs. Fox*, whereby a third-party beneficiary has an enforceable right; this is known as a "chose in action" and is equivalent to an asset.

Another problem arose when Aeolian-Skinner was accused of using nonunion workers. Through its AFL-CIO employees, Miller and Company, an organ manufacturer in Hagerstown, Md., objected strenuously to the gift on these grounds. I took the problem to George Meany,* the AFL-CIO president whom I had come to know as a fellow trustee of the Center, and to his personal representative, Al Zack. They concurred that the organ was a direct gift over which the union had no control, and Meany so informed the Hagerstown local.

Other donations required similar legal attention. The Reynolds Aluminum Company pledged $85,000 worth of aluminum ingot, which could be furnished to a fabricator and made into materials for use in the building. The same was true of cement from Martin Marietta. Entered on the books as pledges, both these contributions were converted into deeds of gift to the satisfaction of GAO and Treasury.

Contributions of $400,000 from the Joseph Kennedy, Jr., Foundation and of $75,000 from the Albert and Mary Lasker Foundation (the first of many the Center would receive through Mary Lasker's repeated acts of generosity) had to be handled diffferently. These had come to us in the form of pledges, and it was necessary to convert them into notes payable to a bank in New York, where the two foundations were domiciled. Under New York law, we would have no problem of enforceability. We accom-

---

* George Meany served on the board of trustees from 1962 through 1974. At the time of his appointment, he said, "This building should not be built for the 'carriage trade' but for 'the people' of the United States," and it was a point he repeated time and time again. While his fellow trustees were generally of the same conviction and adopted policies to enforce it, Meany was clearly the most watchful and vocal "representative of the people" on the board. Another AFL-CIO leader of great help to the Center in these early days was Andrew J. Biemiller, the director of legislation.

plished this through an arrangement worked out through the correspondent bank in Washington, American Security and Trust.

Royalties on books and recordings presented a minor problem because we had been carrying them on our books as accounts receivable. Happily, GAO ruled favorably on them, permitting us to show them as assets. All told, however, the amount earned in royalties before the June deadline came to only $35,000—$30,000 from two corporate advertisers in *Creative America*, the book on American artists published in 1962, and $5,000 from RCA from sales of the military bands recordings.

It took us a bit more time to turn an Andrew Wyeth painting into an acceptable asset. The Center had been given the painting with the understanding that proceeds from its sale would be shared with the American Shakespeare Festival. An auction held the year before, however, had brought a high bid of only $45,000, which officials of both the Center and the Shakespeare Festival refused, convinced that the painting was worth a great deal more. Fortunately, they turned out to be right. The painting was later sold for considerably more money and the proceeds split in time to meet our deadline.

By April the remaining pledges amounted to $1,606,014, and the Executive Committee concluded that there was little or no chance of redeeming them before the deadline. Thus, we began to think earnestly about other, faster ways they might be turned into cash.

With Stevens's approval, I sought the counsel of Robert Fleming, chairman of the board of Riggs National Bank. Fleming had every right to be miffed with the Center since all our deposits were in American Security. Much to my relief, he listened warmly and sympathetically, said he would be pleased to do whatever he could, and promptly turned me over to his attorneys, Hogan and Hartson. Thereupon the Center got a lucky break. John Warner, then of Hogan and Hartson and later a U.S. senator (R-Va.), was assigned to the project.

Robert C. Baker, the chief operating officer at American Security, was informed of my meeting with Fleming. With Baker's blessing, Warner immediately initiated discussions with the firm of Shea and Gardner, attorneys for American Security. During the first of these, I proposed that the two banks buy the pledges under an arrangement that would give the Center an option to repurchase, thereby enabling us to protect whatever equity we had. The idea seemed attractive and, as discussions progressed, got more specific: The Center would sell pledges amounting to $1,220,000 and hold the balance ($400,000) in reserve to cover contingencies, notably the anticipated nonpayment of some pledges. As for the time during which the Center would have an option to repurchase, I suggested five years.

Benjamin W. Boley was the Shea and Gardner lawyer representing American Security. He worried that the Center might not have the authority to enter into the type of agreement I was proposing, and he questioned the Center's performance ability, especially whether it would be able to complete construction as planned. But his chief concern was the nature of the pledges and their enforceability in a court of law. To reduce the risk, he recommended that American Security require additional collateral—$500,000 in new pledges when they came in. Warner's position was that the public interest was implicated and that the normal standards of a commercial transaction simply did not apply.

Shea and Gardner grew adamant and remained so. On June 23 negotiations reached an impasse. Acutely aware that it was C-Day minus seven, Warner advised me to have Stevens speak directly with Robert Baker.[2] That same day I wrote Stevens a memorandum outlining the problem as I saw it. After hearing from Stevens, Baker told his lawyers to back off. On June 29, just one day before deadline, the sale-and-repurchase agreement was consummated.

None of Benjamin Boley's fears was realized. By January 31, 1967, the Center had enough funds to pay the two banks $53,058 in accrued charges and to buy back $674,564 in pledges. Only a few of these pledges—fewer than 1 percent—were never collected or proved uncollectible, almost all because the donors died without making bequests.

At the same time that the sale-and-repurchase agreement was being negotiated, we were trying to get all the foreign gifts assessed and their value approved by GAO and Treasury. Of these, the marble donated by Italy undoubtedly got the most attention. The Italian government had appropriated $600,000 for the marble's acquisition, but architect Stone maintained that when honed and polished it would be worth almost double that

* Baker was named treasurer of the Center in 1968, serving until 1972.

amount—to be precise, $1,132,000.* Treasury accepted Stone's valuation, thereby making an exception to its otherwise rigid rule that foreign gifts could go on the Center's books only in the amounts appropriated by the donor governments. In accord with this rule, we were credited with $250,000 for West Germany's gift (announced as bronze-and-glass doors but later changed to a large bronze outdoor sculpture); $155,000 for the furniture from Denmark; $180,000 for the 11 Hadelands chandeliers from Norway; and $70,000 for the stage curtain from Japan (about half its market value).

So we met our deadline. On June 30 the Center's accountant, John Addabbo, certified to the comptroller general that our assets included $12 million in cash; $1,112,000 in real estate and property; $1,787,000 in foreign gifts; and $1,317,000 in stocks, and notes or accounts receivable. To be exact, we had raised, all told, $16,322,274.11—almost a million dollars more than the sum we needed to qualify for matching federal dollars.

WITH THE PROSPECT that money would soon be available for construction, I began to busy myself full time in an effort to complete the assembly of land, something I had been working on intermittently for several years. As already noted, an irregular, boomerang-shaped site of 7.5 acres had been specified in the legislative proceedings, but the architect's plan called for a little more than 17 acres. It was a Herculean task to put all this together, and it took eight years. Many obstacles had to be hurdled before construction could begin; and even after the construction contract was let in 1966, many crises over land had to be resolved before the Center opened in 1971.

The NCPC was the statutory agency authorized to acquire land and assemble the necessary property, and the legislation that created the Center specified that the land be bought with funds available "for parks and parkway services as part of the National Park System." For us, this proved to be an unforeseen and welcome dividend. What it meant was that, once acquired, the property became part of the Rock Creek and Potomac Parkway of the NPS, a circumstance that enabled Park Service officials to

---

* Shipment was the gift of the Isbrandtsen Lines, the cost of which was not converted to an asset for matching purposes.

participate actively in making Center plans and policies. This they did in an unfailingly positive spirit, which was never more manifest or appreciated than when they realized for the first time that to make room for the Center the parkway would have to be moved closer to the Potomac seawall.

The NCPC had Capper-Crampton funds to buy private lands. The other land to be assembled either was owned by or came under the jurisdiction of various agencies of the U.S. and District governments, and only deeds of transfer were required. But acquisition of the private properties was an entirely different matter, and negotiations hardly went as smoothly. After dragging on for several years, the problem had reached the critical stage by February 1965. Daniel Shear, NCPC's general counsel, made this abundantly clear in a letter advising me that

> there are three properties in private ownership. The commission has negotiated a land purchase contract for Lot 802 in Square 11, owned by Adele M. Ward, in the amount of $90,000. . . . Lot 5 in Square 11, and lots 1 through 3 and 8 through 12 inclusive in Square 12, are titled in Christian Heurich, Jr., and Charles Ellison Eckles, surviving trustees under the will of Christian Heurich deceased. Messrs. Heurich and Eckles have indicated their willingness to sell the properties at $40 per square foot or $2,039,040 for the 50,976 square feet therein. . . . The remaining property is the Watergate Inn owned by Mrs. Marjorie Hendricks. Messrs. Savage and Donohoe appraised the property at $450,000 and $432,000, respectively, in October of 1962.

Acquiring the Watergate Inn property proved troublesome. There was, Shear reported, an outstanding though questionable contract of sale for $900,000 on the property, held by that predatory syndicate (see chap. 5) formed in anticipation of an offer from the NCPC. Through Mrs. Hendricks's attorney, James C. Wilkes, the NCPC tried to negotiate a direct purchase, offering between $450,000 and $700,000, but failed. Accordingly, in September condemnation proceedings were brought by the Department of Justice, accompanied by an allowance of $450,000 for the quarter acre. Mrs. Hendricks promptly countered with a suit challenging the legality of the government's action. Ultimately, Justice raised the allowance to $650,000 and the matter was settled.

The Heurich property to which Shear referred was the residue of a historic landmark dating from 1895. Originally the lots had been part of an entire block (25th, 26th, D, and Water streets, N.W.) owned by Christian Heurich, Sr., a German-born immigrant who, long before he died in 1946 at age 102, had become Washington's best-known and probably wealthiest businessman. On this site, for more than 60 years, the Christian Heurich Brewery Company manufactured the District's most popular beers, and one of America's most honored—the recipient of bronze, silver, and gold medals at exhibitions in Paris and Liège.

Three fires in less than five years, however, had destroyed Heurich's first brewery, and to prevent a recurrence he built the Foggy Bottom complex—a bottling plant, an icehouse, and warehouses in addition to the malt mill—of solid concrete, with walls and foundations so thick they could withstand anything but dynamite. In 1952, Heurich's heirs stopped making beer, prompted by two circumstances: (1) nearly lethal competition from Schlitz, Schaeffer, Anheuser-Busch, and other large national breweries; and (2) the demand of the federal government for a big chunk of the land for the approaches to the Theodore Roosevelt Memorial Bridge. The government, however, did not actually condemn and acquire the land until 1961, and during this time the family rented the buildings, primarily for storage. Indeed, Mr. Heurich had built them so solidly that they could not easily be converted to any other purpose.* When wreckers came in the fall of 1961 to tear down the icehouse, they used 650 sticks of dynamite on their first try and succeeded in bringing down only three walls. Next spring, the main brewery building was razed with even more difficulty.

At the time we were acquiring land for the Center, the Heurich family still retained two parcels, separated by E Street. Both fronted on New Hampshire Avenue, and on one of them Stone had sited the Opera House. Without them, the Center simply could not proceed as planned.

The generosity of the Heurich heirs eased our problem, but to actually gain title took time and more than a little ingenuity. There was no disagreement about the value of the lots; NCPC's expert appraisers, Robert W. Savage and Milburn J. Donohoe, Jr., valued them at about the same

---

* One of them, however, was turned into a temporary theater, for a while housing Arena Stage, Washington's now famous resident repertory company.

figure for which the estate's trustees had told Shear the family would sell them. Our problem boiled down to this: Although lawyers for the brewery and the Heurich estate (Cameron Burton and George Schweitzer) were disposed to help, their fiduciary obligation to the heirs mandated that the property be sold for nothing less than "fair market value." The fair market value had been fixed at $2,039,040, but the NCPC had only about $1,900,000 for the purchase, and under the Kennedy Center statute the Center's trustees were obligated to make up the difference. Therefore, unless the Heurich heirs could be persuaded to take a loss or to make a considerable donation, the Center would have to come up with about $140,000, which we didn't have.

For help, I turned to my friend Jan (Mrs. Benjamin C.) Evans, a granddaughter of Mr. and Mrs. Christian Heurich, Sr. She introduced me to her uncle, Charles Eckles, and a long, favorable conference followed. Both he and the other surviving trustee, his brother-in-law Christian Heurich, Jr., told me that "it was not a question of finance." They would be willing to take a loss, they said, if necessary, as a way of contributing to the Center.

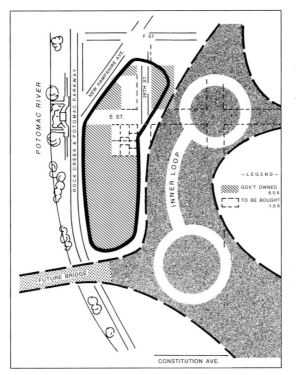

The "boomerang" site provided for in the 1958 National Cultural Center Act was approximately 7.5 acres, about 10 acres shy of the number needed to site the building in the parklike setting prescribed by Stone's plans. Before the Center could be built, 17.5 acres of land had to be assembled. Shaded areas indicate parcels acquired from private owners, the most critical of which was the old Heurich Brewery.

95

They reminded me, however, that they were barred from disposing of the property for less than market value. They then volunteered that they would consider any reasonable proposal that did not require the family to put up cash.

I proposed that they make a gift of this quarter acre, valued at $150,000, in exchange for two boxes, one in the Opera House and one in the Concert Hall. They said they were interested and would take it up with their counsel.

Shortly thereafter the family's attorneys advised us that a conveyance of 3,750 square feet of land would be made to the Center if we could ensure its approval by the Internal Revenue Service as a $150,000 tax deductible contribution. I immediately got in touch with IRS commissioner Sheldon Cohen, explained our problem, and a few days later met with him and the director of the tax rulings division, John W. B. Littleton. In a letter to Littleton dated May 4, 1965, I requested a ruling, noting the amounts of the two appraisals, reviewing the Center's legislative history, and enclosing a legal memorandum. I was careful to point out that under provisions of the statute, "the Board is authorized to solicit and accept . . . and to hold and administer gifts . . . of money, securities, or *any other property of whatsoever character."*

After retaining its own appraiser, the IRS responded expeditiously and favorably by letter directly to the heirs. The letter was dated May 25, which was 35 days before C-Day. Earlier, the family had agreed to sell the remainder of the needed property to the NCPC at an appropriate figure of $1,900,000; this, with the $150,000 tax credit, brought income from the sale up to fair market value, thus satisfying all obligations to the heirs. Once the land was transferred from the NCPC to the Center, we became entitled to a like credit of $150,000 in matching funds.

A ceremony was held on June 23, 1965, at which time the three Heurich heirs presented Stevens with the deed. As agreed, we accepted the gift as a memorial to Mr. and Mrs. Christian Heurich, Sr. Their names are now attached to two presidential boxes, one in the Opera House and one in the Concert Hall.

There were five tenants on the Heurich parcels to be relocated. We had a problem with only one of them. Notwithstanding condemnation proceedings, Luke Vandergrift, proprietor of the Washington Diner at 2610

E Street, refused to vacate unless compensated for his loss. He managed to hold up excavation as late as October 1966, when the NCPC settled with him.

With condemnation in September of Marjorie Hendricks's Watergate property, the acquisition of private lands was complete. Our work to secure the site, however, was far from over, for now we had to cope with the complex problems of closing streets and alleys in the area. A difficult job under any circumstance, it was made all the more difficult by our persistent critics, who seized upon it as a pretext to renew their objections to the Potomac setting.

This time there were many new faces among our adversaries: Reps. Charles McC. Mathias, Jr. (R-Md.) and Thomas B. Curtis (R-Mo.), and Sen. Karl Mundt (R-S.D.). They kept at us almost without letup from late August 1965 until well into 1966. However well intentioned, they put us under a constant barrage of false and erroneous statements. Now, to their old charges and tactics they added a proposal that the Center be moved to Pennsylvania Avenue. It took all our guns to fend them off.

The campaign started with a statement from Nicholas Satterlee, president of the American Institute of Architects. He had "received information," he said, that the Temporary Commission on Pennsylvania Avenue was recommending relocation of the Center to Pennsylvania Avenue. This was denied by Daniel Patrick Moynihan, the commission's vice chairman (and later a Democratic senator from New York), who said plainly that the commission had never made such a recommendation, nor did it have any such intent. As far as he was concerned, the issue had been settled. We double-checked with Edward T. Foote, assistant to the chairman. He too believed that the matter was settled. He added that there was no space large enough on Pennsylvania Avenue to accommodate the Center. I called Charles A. Horsky, adviser to the president on capital affairs, who reassured me of White House support for our site.

Even so, this marked the beginning of a new fire on the Potomac River. As might have been expected, the fire was lit by our old critics: Widnall, Frain, and Immer. On August 12, Widnall introduced a bill to set up a commission to reconsider the site. A week later, he introduced another bill, this one to relocate the Center to Pennsylvania Avenue. Unhappily, he received considerable support.

Once again, Stevens and others on the board fought to bring our case to the public. We reminded our critics that the architect had positioned the Center in a parklike environment, a traditional setting for memorials in Washington. The chosen site took maximum advantage of the river in the same sensible way that the Houses of Parliament made use of the Thames and the Louvre used the Seine. The Potomac River and Theodore Roosevelt Island formed a vista of natural beauty—an uninterrupted vista, moreover, since the river terrace of the Center would be above the Rock Creek and Potomac Parkway.

Beyond its aesthetics, we focused on the site's practical advantages, meeting head-on those opponents who stressed its inaccessibility. We pointed out that the Watergate concerts, which had been a popular river attraction long before the Center was planned, never suffered from a lack of attendance, and they were held in a setting less well served by access routes than the Center would be. We argued, I think convincingly, that easy vehicular access from Maryland and the District would be provided by the Inner Loop Freeway from New Hampshire Avenue, and from the Virginia side by the Memorial, Roosevelt, and Key bridges. Further, the planned extension of freeways and parkways radially through the city and its environs—with connections to the Inner Loop Freeway, the Capital Beltway, and, eventually, an outer beltway—promised to make the Center even more accessible to suburban Maryland and Virginia.

A word more about this projected system of roadways: It constitutes still another example of President Eisenhower's vision and of his contribution to the domestic welfare, so generally unrecognized. Part of one of the largest public works in our history, it was a creature of the Federal Highway Act, commonly called the Interstate and Defense Highway Act, which the president had signed into law on June 29, 1956. To his foresight we owe our first truly nationwide highway system, today a 42,500-mile network serving more than 90 percent of American cities with populations of more than 50,000.*

Since the Washington component of this system skirted the downtown area, the river location we favored would be more accessible to more

* Remarkably, this pay-as-you-go system has been built and maintained without any necessity to draw on the general fund of the Treasury; 90 percent of the costs have been paid by the federal government's Highway Trust Fund, the remaining 10 percent by the states.

On September 29, 1965, as excavation was about to begin, Stevens climbed aboard a derrick and flashed a confident smile. Unhappily, it was not enough to convince critics that the Center "meant business."

people than any possible site on Pennsylvania Avenue. This was not our own conclusion but that of the NCPC and the NPS, both of which sponsored studies confirming it, as well as that of the D.C. government and of various independent consultants. Actual time tests were conducted in 1965 of traffic on streets leading from such spots as Dupont Circle, the National Cathedral, and the Mayflower Hotel. Without exception, these tests showed it easier to reach the Center than the National Theatre on Pennsylvania Avenue.

Clearly, too, parking facilities at the Center would be far superior to the on-street parking necessary for any proposed Pennsylvania Avenue site. Stone's design called for 12 traffic lanes entering and leaving from various directions. Seven hundred feet of covered space was provided for passenger debarkation.

Our success in raising private contributions in the volume necessary to earn matching federal funds earned us some favorable publicity and undoubtedly brought more public support for our case. Radiating confidence, in September Stevens held a press conference on Rock Creek Parkway. "We're going ahead," he said, and climbed a derrick to emphasize his point.

THERE WERE SOME, HOWEVER, who thought Stevens was merely whistling a happy tune. Shortly before the press conference, Representative Curtis had introduced a joint resolution intended to stop construction of the Center for at least 90 days, pending a study by the NCPC of "the relative merits of the present site on the Potomac." Curtis said the review process would take into account the views of all interested and competent parties, and especially the "views of President Kennedy's immediate family, who are understandably distressed over the present site." He reminded Congress that President Franklin D. Roosevelt's family had successfully stopped the "Stonehenge" memorial planned near the Tidal Basin.

Curtis was a powerful figure and the second-ranking Republican on the House Ways and Means Committee. An old friend of mine, he sincerely felt that the considerable controversy over the site had caused enough criticism to justify full public investigation, especially in view of the new plans for Pennsylvania Avenue, for a subway system, and for downtown urban renewal funds. On September 27, I wrote him a long letter, giving him the facts and recounting the Center's legislative history, to which I attached a memorandum on the role of the NCPC. I pointed out the mistakes in his press release, knowing Curtis to be a man of honesty and integrity who would take my criticisms in the right spirit. I took particular pains to remind him that Mrs. Jacqueline Kennedy, Sen. Robert F. Kennedy, and Mrs. Jean Kennedy Smith were all active members of our board of trustees and that, contrary to the statement in his press release, none of them had ever criticized the river site.

Curtis was convinced. He made it clear that he would go no further in his opposition to the Potomac River site, and he withdrew from any further action on his resolution. What's more, he said that it was a waste of time and unnecessary to change the site. From that point on, he supported legislation for the Center in every respect.

I also wrote Representative Mathias, enclosing a memorandum similar to the one I'd sent Curtis. On October 5, 1965, Mathias responded:

> I regret that a misunderstanding seems to have developed between us on the question of the Kennedy Center site. I do not condemn the present site, nor do I endorse any specific alternative. I do believe, however, that it is prudent to provide an outlet for criti-

cism of the present plans now, rather than undermining public
support for the Center by forcing dissent to continue to run
underground.

In my subsequent conversations with him, he withdrew his opposition.

I took a similar approach with Senator Mundt, enclosing in my letter
a memorandum, a chronology, and documentary exhibits dealing with the
participation of the NCPC in the site selection. Mundt reevaluated his
position as well. He stated:

> I am quite content to leave it to others to make the final
> adjudications, and I assure you that I do not want to get any more
> deeply involved in any controversy which might involve you. I am
> now quite content to retire from the arena.

Mundt said further that he would do nothing to interfere with the construction of the Center. Indeed, he promised to be helpful in every way possible,
and he was.

Widnall then tried to enlist the support of Rep. George D. Fallon
(D-Md.), the chairman of the House Public Works Committee. Fallon
reviewed his committee's position, found that it had consistently supported the Potomac site, and let it be known that, as far as he was concerned, the issue was closed. Referring to the extensive hearings and to the
fact that all interested parties had had ample opportunity to air their views,
he went on to emphasize that "hundreds of individuals and organizations,
in addition to foreign governments, have or will contribute to the Center
and made their commitments on the basis of the present site, thereby
giving tacit approval." The *Washington Star* agreed with Fallon and
expressed the hope that "his decision, which is eminently sound, will
officially end this fruitless controversy once and for all."

The Center brought out its blockbusters—the three Senate trustees
of the Center—Saltonstall, Fulbright, and Clark. On September 30, 1965, all
three spoke out forcefully on the Senate floor in favor of the Potomac River
site. Our critics, however, were undeterred. On October 15, 1965, "A Peti-
tion Relating to the Location of the Center" appeared as a half-page adver-
tisement in the *Washington Post.* Signed by 144 prominent individuals, it
asked for a 60-day moratorium and for a review committee to "hear, study,

and make recommendations concerning all questions relating to the location of the Center."

Roger Stevens released a 14-page reply addressed to three of the signers representing influential interest groups: Mrs. W. John Kenney, E. Fulton Brylawski, and Adm. Neill Phillips. His memorandum was faithfully summarized by Richard L. Coe, the *Post*'s drama critic, in his column of October 21, and after that, serious opposition to the site ceased.

Nevertheless, the battle had generated a lot of animosity and misunderstanding, and Stevens concluded that we needed to present the public with incontrovertible evidence of progress. As a consequence, we redoubled our efforts to complete land assemblage, a task that by this time principally involved arranging for the closing of some 4.3 acres of streets and alleys, including parts of New Hampshire Avenue and Northwest D and E streets.

These proposed closings were on land that abutted property held entirely by the U.S. and District governments. The closings were necessary both to facilitate construction of the Center and to ensure a "parklike setting." We thought it essential to show that, from the outset, Congress and the D.C. Board of Commissioners had intended to authorize the closing of streets and alleys. The commissioners had approved the river site because it allowed for appropriate ingress and egress, and early congressional hearings had made it clear that the land we needed to have vacated was adjacent to the statutory site. The NCPC was also on record as approving the closings.

In testimony before the NCPC in early December I noted that time was of the essence. GSA had already let a demolition contract; even as I spoke, a contractor was demolishing buildings on the Center site. GSA had also awarded a contract for excavation. Moreover, under a $1 million contract let by the NPS, work was proceeding on relocation of the parkway. GSA's review of final plans and drawings with the architect and engineers contemplated an early bid for the general construction contract.

Conferences with D.C. officials proved fruitful. The Department of Traffic had no objections to the closings. The corporation counsel's office was supportive. By letter to the architect, the chief of the Department of Sanitary Engineering gave approval on condition that existing water and sewer facilities be preserved. Our persistent critics, however, once again were not subdued. Now they charged that closing New Hampshire Avenue would deprive taxpayers of public space, a criticism I thought frivolous and groundless. Once the parkway was relocated, public access to and egress from New Hampshire Avenue and E Street to the parkway would no longer exist; after that, there would simply be no need for such access or egress, whether New Hampshire Avenue was vacated or not.

At issue was who had the right to file a valid objection as a party of interest. My contention was that the only parties of interest were the owners of abutting land. The U.S. government and its relevant agencies all concurred. By this rationale, Frain, Immer, and Widnall were not parties of interest and therefore had no right to file objections. It was on this premise that the D.C. commissioners later ruled in favor of the Center after a supporting opinion was rendered by Judge Milton Korman as corporation counsel.

The objection of owners of the Watergate project was of greater concern because their land abutted New Hampshire Avenue. In response, at a December hearing of the Zoning Commission, I used the presentation that the owners themselves had made before that same commission four years earlier, in which they had acknowledged having been notified of the intent to vacate New Hampshire Avenue from F Street to the parkway. And to bolster my argument, I submitted the site plan of the National Cultural Center that had been approved by the NCPC as early as December 3, 1959; it too had projected closings on New Hampshire Avenue. Not long thereafter, whether because of my argument or not, the developers withdrew their objections.

On December 29, the D.C. commissioners gave the order to close the necessary streets and alleys, as they found the closings

> just and equitable in view of all circumstances of the case affecting nearby property of abutters and/or non-abutters under the provision permitting closing by reason of acquisition by the United States for public purposes of all the property abutting on the streets and alleys proposed to be closed. Title to all the property abutting on the streets and alleys proposed to be closed is in the United States and the use proposed—construction of the Kennedy Center—is clearly a public purpose. The Commissioners, therefore, have the authority to close the streets and alleys in question.

On February 4, 1966, by order of the D.C. commissioners, the NCPC was authorized to effect consent transfers whereby the Center's board of trustees would be given title to the building, and the park surrounding it would be put under jurisdiction of the NPS. It looked, therefore, as if we were now able to move ahead without further harassment.

But no. Three months before, John Immer had written Atty. Gen. Nicholas deB. Katzenbach, contending that it was illegal to extend the boundaries of the Center to the seawall of the Rock Creek and Potomac Parkway and to relocate the parkway. Widnall had transmitted a copy of this letter to Roger Stevens, who had responded quickly and forcefully to the effect that although opponents would never be satisfied, the Center was going to be built nevertheless. Thereupon Widnall had begun agitating every agency and department of the federal and district governments with the slightest interest in the Center, as well as virtually every radio and television station in town. A rumor, given great currency by the *Washington Post*, circulated that construction of the relocated parkway had been stopped. This was not true, although Immer did threaten an injunction.

This last major site issue was resolved, finally, on February 15, 1966, when Edward Weinberger, acting solicitor of the Interior Department, sent a memo to Edwin L. Weisl, Jr., assistant attorney general, Lands and Resources Division, who was in charge of the relocation. In it, Weinberger answered specific questions about the authority of the Center's trustees to construct the building partially outside the statutory site and concluded that "the Congressional actions with respect to the Kennedy Center subsequent to the 1958 authorization had the effect of modifying the original boundaries of the site." Weisel agreed, and that was that.

It took four more years to complete the assembly of all the access roads. In fact, the final transfer—conveyance by the D.C. government of a parcel affecting access to the Theodore Roosevelt Bridge from the parkway—was not accomplished until the fall of 1971, only a week or so before the Center formally opened. All the same, by the end of 1965, we had enough land for work to begin.

And begin it did.

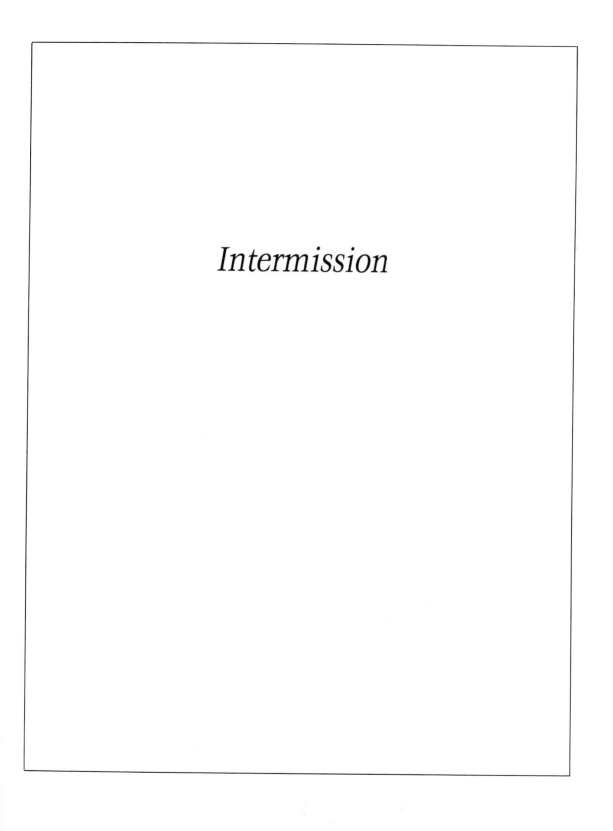

Intermission

Going up!

In a "topping off" ceremony in January 1968, an 11-foot steel reproduction of a violincello was hoisted to the top of the Concert Hall. The replica was autographed by maestro Erich Leinsdorf just before its ascent.

In September giant copies of the Greek masks for comedy and tragedy were sent to the top of what a month later would be christened the Eisenhower Theater.

To fashion exterior walls, a thin skin of marble was attached to seven inches of bonded reinforced concrete. By summer 1969, one third of the marble was in place.

*The Concert Hall
under construction,
August 1968.*

*The Concert Hall,
Standing Room Only,
1972; a timpanist's eye
view. The 11 Hadelands
chandeliers were a gift
from Norway.*

In Performance

Itzhak Perlman has performed at the Center almost every year since 1972.

*Isaac Stern in rehearsal...
and in concert.*

Before his death in 1973, cellist Pablo Casals appeared in the Concert Hall as both soloist and conductor. With him is his wife, Marta, now married to the distinguished pianist Eugene Istomin. Since 1980 Ms. Istomin has been the Center's artistic director.

Maestro Mstislav Rostropovich. When he turned 60 in 1987 the Center honored him with a gala during which Mrs. Reagan took the baton and led the National Symphony in "Happy Birthday." The occasion also marked his 10th anniversary as the symphony's music director.

On the Eisenhower stage some very old plays...

Richard Chamberlain in Richard II, *with Patrick Hines, Jack Ryland, and Sorell Booke. (May 3-22, 1972)*

Zoe Caldwell and Dame Judith Anderson in Medea. *(March 3- April 10, 1982.)*

And some
not so old...

*George Grizzard as
Tony Cavendish in*
The Royal Family, *with
James Burge and
Mark Fleischman.
(November 11-
December 13, 1975)*

Elizabeth Taylor and Alexander Zerbe in The
Little Foxes. *(March 17-April 26, 1981)*

Jason Robards and Leonardo Cimino in The
Iceman Cometh. *(July 31-September 14, 1985)*

Opera

The Opera House production of Ariodante (September 14, 1971), with Beverly Sills in the leading role, marked the first time Handel's great opera had been staged in the United States.

Yoko Watanabe as Cio-Cio-San in the Washington Opera production of Madama Butterfly. (November 20-29, 1987)

The throne room from La Scala's Simon Boccanegra. (September 7-19, 1976)

The St. Basil scene from Boris Godunov, *produced by the Bolshoi Opera.*
(July 22- August 3, 1975)

Ballet

Vladimir Vasiliev of the Bolshoi in Giselle. *(May 28, 1975)*

Mikhail Baryshnikov and Marianna Tcherkassky in the
American Ballet Theatre production of Le Spectre de
la Rose. *(March 30, 1976)*

Musical Plays

Craig Schulman as Jean Valjean in Les Miserables. *(December 29, 1986-February 14, 1987)*

Angela Lansbury in Sweeney Todd. *(October 26-November 29, 1980)*

Mickey Rooney and Linda Michele in Show Boat. *(May 7-19, 1974)*

Annie *(Andrea McCardle), orphans, and Sandy. (March 1-April 2, 1977)*

Scott Joplin's opera Treemonisha. *(September 3-21, 1975)*

And all that jazz...

The New Orleans Preservation Hall Jazz Band. (March 17, 1977)

7

CONSTRUCTION:
The Miracle Takes Shape

*E*dward Durell Stone's design for the Center evolved through several mutations. Originally, plans called for a roof studio theater of 450 seats, and a tourist center with a 200-seat cinema. Both were eliminated as we moved along, the first because there was no reasonable way to shield the auditorium from aircraft noise, the second for reasons of expense. By spring 1965, after all refinements, the superstructure was defined as 300 feet by 630 feet by 69 feet high, plus a penthouse of 230 feet by 560 feet by 26 feet high. The exterior was to be exposed to its best advantage from "E" Street, New Hampshire Avenue, Rock Creek Parkway, and the Theodore Roosevelt Bridge; the roads from the entrance plaza were to be screened at eye level by hedges. The finished building would contain the Eisenhower Theater (1,150 seats), the Opera House (2,250 seats), the Concert Hall (2,750 seats), the Terrace Theater* (500 seats), the Theater Lab (250 seats), the American Film Institute Theater (224 seats), and the Grand Foyer, the largest hall in the world. Each hall and theater was planned to accommodate performing arts of all types. In addition, large atriums were planned that would provide space, as needed, for meetings, lectures, and special performances. The Kennedy Center was to be the first facility in the world to house several performance halls, dining areas, garages, and several hundred offices under one roof.

Stone's aesthetic vision did much to sustain us while we went about

---

* Designed by Philip Johnson and John Burgee and constructed in 1979, the Terrace Theater was donated by Japan as a bicentennial gift to America. The gift was arranged by Harold Burson of the public relations firm Burson-Marsteller.

the business of fund raising and land acquisition. During those anxious days we were given many occasions to review and discuss the plans, and the prospect of what the Center could be never failed to excite us. As early as spring 1964, following a presentation by landscape architects Hideo Sasaki and Edward Stone, Jr., the NCPC's Federal Planning and Projects Committee approved the site plan. Edward Durell Stone presented his plans to the board a few months later (to be exact, on July 22), at which time we gave formal approval to his concept. After that, even as we continued to be engrossed with problems of land assembly, we began to draft contracts for construction.

Drafting the contracts for so complicated a project was not easy. In the basic architectural engineering (A/E) contract between Stone and the Center, the services of many ad hoc specialists—site investigation engineers, acoustical engineers, and landscape architects, as well as consultants

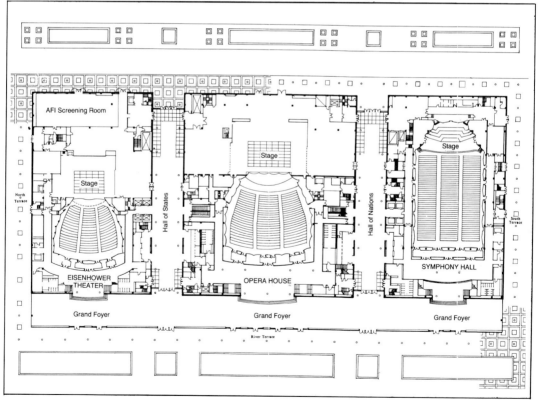

Plan of plaza level and orchestras.

in stage design, lighting, seating, and parking—had to be specified and provided for. Negotiating terms satisfactory to GSA, the architect, and Center officials was a long and complex process, during which I worked closely with GSA. The contract was consummated on August 10 under terms that set the A/E fee at $2,128,000—approximately 5.25 percent of the Center's estimated cost, a standard rate for such complex structures. This sum included a credit to the Center of $211,677, the amount already paid Stone for work completed. (The Center's $391,676 payment to Stone for his first concept and developmental plans was excluded.)

On December 2, 1964, the board of trustees met three times—in the Treaty Room of the Executive Office Building, at the Center site, and in the John Quincy Adams Room of the State Department. At each meeting, GSA gave us an up-to-date estimate of construction costs: $45,579,000. We were told that Stone would submit final plans by March 30, 1965. By this same timetable, bidding was to begin on May 1 and GSA was to award the general contract in June.

The date would be missed by almost one year.

At the trustees' meeting that followed, on May 17, 1965, Stone made a brief presentation of the architectural plans and showed us 3/8-inch-scale models of the interiors of the four theaters. He reported that except for the administrative areas, architectural planning was complete; there had been no substantial change in either concept or facilities since our meeting the previous July. About the only change worth noting, in fact, was the addition of a separate presidential and VIP entrance from the parkway, the plan for which had been worked out after consultations with the U.S. Secret Service and other security agencies. He then ended his presentation by expressing his concern, one we all shared, over the proximity and height of the Watergate apartment development north of the Center. He hoped every effort would be made to diminish its height or to create a park in its place.

Three days before, GSA had issued a new project directive estimating building costs at $43,741,500. Our anticipated and available funds were $43,450,000. To be sure, the new figure was lower than earlier estimates, but even so there was still a deficit of $291,500. Clearly, we had to make further cuts, and among the alternatives submitted for our consideration were these:

1. Substitute colored aluminum for bronze
   on exterior column covers $200,000

2. Eliminate Studio Theater $1,029,000

3. Eliminate architectural finishes and
   mechanical work in multipurpose area $256,000

At the same time, we discussed desirable items for which no funds were available. These included:

1. Auditorium projection and sound systems $309,000

2. Special stage lighting and fixtures $121,000

3. Furniture and furnishings, including
   carpeting and stage curtains $750,000

4. Landscape planting $300,000

The May 14 project directive was approved with various alternatives and deferrals.

At the 1966 annual meeting, on February 7, we considered terms for the general construction contract. Of much importance, we agreed to write in a cost ceiling, a firm fixed fee, and a deadline for completion, all of which we saw as incentives for the contractor and protection for the Center. Negotiating such a contract would not be easy, Stevens told us, and it would be further complicated by the design demands peculiar to a performing arts theater; these would require at least $2 million in separate contracts. Moreover, because plans and specifications could not spell out everything in detail, Stevens and GSA anticipated a lot of change orders in the course of construction and unpredictable cost increases as a consequence.

In view of all this, Stevens said that he and GSA's Design and Construction Division had decided it would be unwise to advertise for bids. The Center was a unique project architecturally, structurally, and aesthetically. Its needs ranged from acoustical engineering (half art, half science); to ballet-friendly stage flooring; to scaffolds and reinforced ceilings for the hanging of 18 crystal chandeliers, each weighing more than a ton; to the tailored accommodation of donated materials from many different sources, produced according to many different standards and measures.

Our needs were simply too special to be subjected to a general bidding process.

The solution, Stevens said, was for the Center to invite bids only from builders and suppliers with earned reputations for both competence and creative problem-solving. Selective bidding would permit us to draw on the special experience of contractors who had constructed similar buildings; bidding costs would be substantially reduced; and, relieved of the obligation to respond to every unsolicited bidder, we would be in a position to award contracts much sooner. Selective bidding also promised to give us better control since it was more likely to attract contractors willing to absorb unanticipated costs as a public service.

At Stevens's direction, I had been conferring with the legal departments of GSA and the comptroller general, and at the time of the annual meeting we were awaiting a ruling that would exempt the Center from the necessity of advertising for bids. The trustees authorized Stevens to proceed to negotiate a contract if GSA and the comptroller general approved.

At this same meeting, on recommendation of the Building Committee, we approved a few design changes, the most painful being to scrub the Tourist Reception Center. According to Stone's original plan, this was to have been located in an area of about 5,000 square feet at the rear of the three stages and was to have included a 200-seat cinema. We decided to leave the space unfinished until we could determine what additional facilities, such as workshops and rehearsal space, we needed.

The hard-working Building Committee functioned as an arm of the Executive Committee and kept separate, detailed minutes of its every action. Members met two or three times a week and were in constant touch with Stevens and me—sometimes every day if they had a particularly acute problem. They followed with great care the work of Oliver Smith and Donald Oenslager, the stage and lighting designers. It was under this committee's scrupulous review that the entire orchestra pit lift, structural supports, and musicians' entrances were redesigned. The committee should also be credited with the installation of television outlet facilities on the second mezzanine level of the Opera House, a recommendation it made in consultation with a task force of television network executives. Had it not been for their vision and for the chief engineer's inspired placement of hidden cameras, today's telecasts of the

Kennedy Center Honors would be much more difficult to produce, if not impossible.

Funding was very much on our minds in the early months of 1966. I became convinced that the anticipated deficit was only a paper one, though I turned out to be wrong. We did need $4 million for the separate contracts, but I expected that the Center would benefit from foreign gifts of fixtures and furniture since negotiations were ongoing with various countries. What made me overly confident was that GAO had approved our use of the federal appropriated funds first, which allowed the Center's invested funds to produce interest income over the next several years. That income would produce a surplus over and above the administrative expenses of the Center, giving us a safety valve in the event that bids were higher than anticipated. I also expected final plans to be completed and ready for bid by April 1966.

The February trustees meeting was an extraordinarily busy one. With respect to furniture, furnishings, and decor, the trustees appointed a special committee made up of Mrs. George Brown and Jean Kennedy Smith, who worked with the Building Committee. The distinguished conductor, Eric Leinsdorf, recommended a second opinion on acoustics, which were critically important. Subsequently, GSA selected Dr. Vern O. Knudsen, chancellor of UCLA. Dr. Knudsen was generally considered to be the dean of U.S. acousticians, and he had, in fact, taught Cyril Harris, the consultant retained by the Center. Harris, who had a provision giving him exclusive credit for acoustical work, objected to our seeking a second opinion and even brought in counsel. Knudsen cheerfully advised that he did not want any credit, and the trustees unanimously supported the chairman's recommendation that GSA continue to use his services. After conducting tests and analyzing the findings, he concurred with Dr. Harris's recommendations. As agreed, he received no credit.

On February 28, 1966, the trustees again met, this time to discuss final plans and specifications, including changes recommended by the program committee aimed at reducing costs. It was an important meeting, and it produced an excellent turnout from members of Congress and NPS representatives. The secretary of the Smithsonian was also present.

The most important item of business was the bidding process. Gratifyingly, the comptroller general had authorized GSA to solicit bids selectively for the general construction contract. This authorization was crucial, and the procedure for getting it was difficult. It required not only an opinion from the comptroller general but also the 100 percent concurrence of the Public Works and Appropriations committees of both the House and the Senate.

Ten firms were selected to submit bids, chosen on the basis of their reliability and experience with similar projects. Of these, eight submitted bids by the June deadline. They included the George Hyman Construction Company; Charles H. Tompkins Company; McCloskey and Company; John McShain Company, Inc.; Turner Company; George A. Fuller Construction Company; Paul Tishman Company; and Pashen-Keiwit.

After we were satisfied that further negotiations would yield no lower bids, we voted to award the general construction contract to the John McShain Company of Philadelphia. The contract was signed on July 26, 1966, with the work to be completed in 865 days. McShain's bid was in most respects the best received. The company bid $249,000 for its fee, including all on-site and off-site supervision and overhead during construction—about one-sixth of its normal bid. As we had hoped, McShain viewed the job as a public service rather than as a strictly profit-making venture. There was, of course, great prestige attached to having received the contract.

In addition to letting the general contract, we entered into agreements for demolition of the site, excavation, and relocating Rock Creek Parkway. At its meeting of October 5, 1966, the Executive Committee approved and ratified the general construction contract. McShain, with GSA's concurrence, then proceeded to solicit bids from subcontractors for steel and electrical work. To our dismay, the two lowest bids were both way over the costs Stone and GSA had estimated in the final project directive. One was 67 percent over and the other, 32 percent. How could this have happened? Immediately, the Building Committee and GSA launched an inquiry. What they found was that material requirements had been spectacularly underestimated; the actual amount of steel needed, for instance, was 47 percent more than the amount on which cost estimates had been based.

Once the situation became apparent, awards were deferred and meetings arranged between Center officers; William Schmidt, the commissioner of public buildings for GSA; and GSA administrator Lawson Knott.

We emphasized that the trustees, and in particular the Building Committee, had at all times relied on the expertise of the architect and GSA, our agent for design and construction supervision. Both Schmidt and Knott were sympathetic and helpful. GSA assumed full responsibility for obtaining a current cost estimate, ascertaining the extent to which the prior estimates may have been understated, and determining the degree to which any differences in costs could have resulted from economic conditions such as increased material and labor costs. Upon the recommendation of GSA and the Building Committee, Stevens authorized an independent outside estimating firm, Michael F. Kenny, Inc., to prepare an accurate cost estimate.

The Executive Committee of the board was informed of these developments at a special meeting on January 23, 1967. We agreed that, upon submission of the report by Kenny, all efforts should be made to determine to what extent, if any, the architect, his engineers and consultants, or GSA were remiss. We also addressed ourselves to the question of the legal remedies available.

MEANWHILE, WE NEEDED TO CONCENTRATE on the subcontractor bids. The discrepancies that had prompted our action in deferring bids had resulted in a new review procedure. Accordingly, requirements and McShain's contract negotiations were scrutinized by a team representing the Center, McShain, and GSA. After substantial negotiations following this revised procedure, a subcontract for steel was awarded to Bethlehem Steel, whose low bid had been $7,255,000. Major electrical work was awarded as a joint venture to E. C. Ernst, Inc., of Washington, D.C., and Fischbach and Moore of New York City, for $5,950,000; mechanical work was awarded to Pierce Associates of Alexandria, Va., for $7,375,000; steel testing work to Gulick-Henderson Laboratories, Inc., of New York for $56,000; reinforcing of steel placement to C. J. Roberts, Inc., of Springfield, Va., for $390,000; fabrication of architectural cast stone to Eastern Schokcrete Corporation of New York for $667,000; and erection of architectural cast stone to Costello Company, Inc., of Cumberland, Md., for $230,000.

Throughout this period, in most business with the Center, GSA was represented by Joseph Moody, its deputy administrator. Moody was the former general counsel for GSA, and no one could have served our interests better. At our board meeting on February 24, 1967, he reported that everything was moving reasonably close to schedule. Excavation work was substantially completed, and 199 of the 340 caissons—58 percent of them—were in place. Consistent with normal GSA experience in major construction projects, the Center presented many problems, but in Moody's opinion, none of them was unique. The Center's most serious problem, he pointed out, was on paper: in several phases of the work, actual costs had exceeded estimates made during the planning stages, but this too was an occurrence not without precedent in the commercial segment of the construction industry. No cost estimate made prior to final completion of the design, he said, could reasonably have been expected to reflect, with any degree of accuracy, the total cost of the facility.

Nevertheless, the cost-estimate differential in our case was uncommonly high, and Moody cited figures. The architect's estimate for the steel required—12,400 tons at $5 million—and the government's estimate—12,800 tons at $5 million—both compared unfavorably with the subcontractor's estimate of 17,000 tons at between $7.7 million and $8.4 million. This was the guts of the issue.

The report from Kenny confirmed the subcontractor's estimate. To be precise, it showed that 16,800 tons of steel were actually required for the building—much more than originally anticipated. Moreover, the Kenny estimate for total construction costs was $55.6 million, for which we had available $49.5 million, a shortage of about $6 million. Sen. Edward Kennedy, speaking as a trustee, asked whether Stone could be held liable. Moody answered that at the time he did not have a basis for an opinion. If, on closer examination, the facts showed that Stone had failed to exercise the degree of care imposed by law in the performance of professional services contracts and that, as a result of such failure, the cost of the project exceeded the limits imposed by contract, Moody thought Stone might have some exposure to liability.*

---

* Later, when we sought further appropriations from Congress, this became a burning issue. At some point, the board decided to withhold the balance of Stone's fee pending resolution of the matter, and once the project was finished Stone sued the Center in an effort to collect. The Center promptly filed a counterclaim. The Justice Department, representing the Center, ultimately worked out a settlement.

Moody closed his board presentation with a recommendation that GSA proceed with construction, which the trustees spiritedly approved. He promised to report back to the Building Committee as soon as GSA had completed its evaluation of the Kenny cost estimate. At that time, he would present the GSA's current best estimate of costs, together with a set of proposals and priorities that would bring total costs within available funding.

In this circumstance, cutting costs was more than essential. One of the more dramatic saving techniques applied was a unique insurance program that used a "wrap-up" approach. Assisted by the expertise of GSA's William Noell and Prof. Herbert Denenberg of the Wharton School of Finance, I developed a unified program that covered the interests of the Center, the prime contractor, and the subcontractors. One of my specialties was insurance, but even so, I relied on Professor Denenberg.

In May 1966, four carefully selected "blue chip" insuring firms—two brokers and two direct writing insurers—were selected to submit insurance proposals. Among the criteria for selection was the ability to write an entire "tailor-made" program. Bidders were sent detailed specifications, prepared by Professor Denenberg, calling for worker's compensation, comprehensive general liability, umbrella liability, builder's risk coverage, ocean marine coverage, performance and payment bonds, officers and trustees' liability, and business interruption coverage.

According to GSA, this integrated program represented the first use by a federal agency of the wrap-up approach to compensation and liability insurance. The wrapup insured not only the constructor (in this case, the Center) but also the contractor and all subcontractors in a single contract, and it added a unified worker's compensation program. Packaging of this sort had inherent economies. As a result, the insurer was able to provide not only substantial cost savings but also better engineering and safety work and more comprehensive protection for all parties.

McShain and all the subcontractors had been advised to exclude insurance from their bids since the Center planned to use the wrap-up approach. As it turned out, all subcontractors, with the exception of Bethlehem Steel, were self-insured and covered for worker's compensation. McShain, however, began the job on site at his own risk pending execution of an insurance program by the Center.

Before GSA could formally give McShain a "Notice to Proceed," procurement regulations required that the contractor be bonded. All members of the Executive and Building committees, along with GSA, unanimously approved the recommendation to place the insurance with Aetna Casualty and Surety Company and participating insurers through the insurance brokerage firm of Johnson and Higgins. Since Aetna had been McShain's insurance carrier in the past, a bond was placed on 24 hours' notice.

We received written proposals in early August 1966 from the four insurance firms and proceeded to evaluate each for cost, coverage, services to be rendered, and the financial strength of the insurer. Johnson and Higgins submitted the least costly proposal and also offered the most comprehensive contract. Its limits were higher, its deductibles lower, and the scope of its protection broader. Such intangibles, in a "tailored" contract, were important but difficult to assess in dollar amounts.

GSA estimated that the insurance placement procedures outlined in my memorandum saved the Center at least $250,000 in premiums. Other estimates ranged as high as $500,000. In any case, the cost of the insurance program was substantially less than what GSA had estimated in its cost-of-project statement.

ON FEBRUARY 15, 1965, a stranger walked into my office and introduced himself as Locke R. Humbert. A man who maintained a very low profile, Humbert was the government relations officer for Pepco, Washington's electric company. The original specifications for the Center had called for steam as the primary source of energy, our assumption being that steam was available at the cheapest rate. In what I later came to know as his characteristically easygoing way, Humbert now asked for an opportunity to show how the Center could save a lot of money by converting to electricity. Although it was a late date to be making a change, I found Humbert persuasive. I discussed the matter, first with Stevens and later with GSA and Stone. They, in turn, talked to Syska and Hennessy, electrical consultants who, at Stone's request, were already investigating alternative power sources.

There ensued a round of conferences among agents of Pepco, GSA, the architect, and the electrical contractor, accompanied by a number of studies, primarily of rate comparisons and of the time-and-dollar costs of the switchover (mostly for redesign of the air-handling and hot-water distribution systems). It finally boiled down to a proposition whereby (1) the Center would agree to use electricity "for the heating requirements of the building, water heating, air conditioning, cooking, general power and lighting"; pay up to $85,000 in conversion costs; and accept a delay of about two months in the submission of final building plans; and (2) Pepco would furnish capital equipment ("the high voltage switchgear, together with the cable from the high voltage switchgear to the transformer vaults" and so on) and guarantee to deliver electricity at a rate competitive with steam. The board accepted the proposal after careful review, resulting in a savings to the Center of about $700,000 in construction costs. The Center thus became "the largest total electric building in the world," a fact happily headlined by Pepco's publicists in July when we announced the conversion.

Potential savings were also a consideration in our solicitation of bids for the food concession. Invitations to bid were sent to interested parties, both locally and nationally. In all cases, such invitations made reference to "public service." For the food concession, we hoped the successful bidder would furnish all the equipment and agree to decorate the facility. We also hoped to be paid at an appropriate time during construction.

The best bid was from the Chicago-based Automatic Canteen Company of America. That company received the exclusive right to sell alcoholic and nonalcoholic beverages, food, candy, cigars, cigarettes, and so on. In return, it agreed to pay the Center $1,250,000, to be applied to the cost of equipping, decorating, furnishing, and supplying the initial expendable inventory. It was agreed further that Automatic Canteen would procure and supervise the installation of all items necessary to equip, furnish, and decorate the facilities, which included a deluxe restaurant and lounge, cafeteria, snack bar, and vending machine services at various locations. Provision was also made for the catering of food and beverages at special events and for beverage service during performance intermissions.

Cumulative costs of installation, equipment, and furnishing amounted to $755,000. Automatic Canteen began reimbursing the Center

The Grand Foyer is the largest room in the world—twice the length of a football field and three times the size of the Hall of Mirrors at Versailles. It serves not only as a lobby for the three main theaters but also as a fourth theater; free musical performances, the most popular being those during the Christmas season, are often staged here. The 18 Orrefors crystal chandeliers were a gift from Sweden.

Since the beginning of President Nixon's second term in January 1973, the Center has been the scene of one of Washington's best attended inaugural balls. Here on the eve of the 1989 inaugural are President Bush and an entourage that included Mr. and Mrs. Bob Hope.

The Hall of Nations and the Hall of States, the two stately entrances to the Grand Foyer. There is room in the Hall of Nations for more flags; it displays those from nations with which the United States currently has diplomatic relations. In the Hall of States is located the gift shop maintained by Friends of the Kennedy Center, an organization of some 600 volunteers.

A $3 million gift from Japan, in commemoration of the American Bicentennial, provided funds for the construction of the Terrace Theater. Designed by Philip Johnson and John Burgee, it opened on January 28, 1979, with a performance of the Grand Kabuki from Tokyo. President Gerald Ford accepted the gift in a Rose Garden ceremony attended by Secretary of State Henry Kissinger (far left) and John Warner, then chairman of the U. S. Bicentennial Commission. A few years earlier, Warner had been instrumental in resolving a critical problem with the Center's funding.

The comfortable and functional American Film Institute Theater will seat 224 confirmed movie addicts.

for these costs in November 1968 and subsequently paid us $495,122 more in reimbursement for the costs of architectural, electrical, and mechanical changes and overhead expenses. This brought their initial commitment up to the $1,250,000 specified in the contract. As of May 13, 1969, the company had expended a total of $905,000. More than $750,000 had gone into brick and mortar.

There were a few problems during the course of completion, however, some with respect to the District of Columbia's inspection control. Although Center officials felt the District had no jurisdiction over federal property, cooperating was one way to ensure satisfactory conditions in compliance with the high standards of excellence contemplated for the concession. Later, Automatic Canteen, which had become a subsidiary of TWA, and the Center mutually agreed to terminate the contract.

Regarding the parking concession, Stevens was interested in "hard cash" to be used for construction and for the best parking plan at the most reasonable fees to the public. The parking facility had been reduced from 1,600 parking spaces to 1,408. We preferred to award this concession, as well as other concessions, to a local firm. APCOA of Washington and Cleveland, however, began negotiating in 1968 and outclassed the entire competition. The negotiating team (Stevens and I) met with the president of APCOA for several months to work out an agreement, and the APCOA contract was executed on February 21, 1969. Under its Parking Concession Agreement, the company advanced the Center $3,500,000, to be repaid from profits over a 15-year period beginning in 1972. It was the company's proposal to provide this advance, which the Center needed to complete construction, and it was an important factor in the selection of a manager for the parking facility. The Center was to share its profits 50-50 until the advance was repaid, at which time the division would be 70 percent to the Center and 30 percent to APCOA. The advance was repaid in 1983. No other proposal came close to the terms proposed by APCOA for an unfinished building.

Trying to save money for the Center often involved time-consuming and difficult negotiations with firms like Pepco, Automatic Canteen, and APCOA. But there were also very pleasurable experiences, as happened with the Sousa Memorial. In 1964, retired colonel George S. Howard, former director of the U.S. Air Force Band, was serving as chairman of the board of directors of the Sousa Memorial Fund. Colonel Howard was head of the music department at Port Chester (New York) High School, my alma mater. The colonel and I knew each other well, and I was pleased when he came to see me in my office, bringing with him James L. Dixon, a businessman, songwriter, and member of the fund's Executive Committee.

Colonel Howard announced that the American Bandmasters Association—comprised largely of high school and college bandmasters, the American School Band Directors Association, and the National Band Association—was interested in memorializing the well-known "March King," John Philip Sousa. Although his name is synonymous with band music since he wrote more than 100 marches, Sousa also composed comic operas, suites, and a symphonic poem. Originally, Howard had in mind a bandshell to be erected on the roof of the Center. This was a great idea because the facility could be used for many other outdoor activities, too. Due to the noise of jets at nearby National Airport, however, the idea was abandoned. Still, Howard and his colleagues had a $100,000 endowment from a nonprofit corporation established in 1956, formed

> for the purpose of memorializing the musician who was the most universally famous of American bandmasters and whose leadership and example have been the motivation and guiding inspiration for bandsmen of today and one of the foundations of modern American bands and band music.

So we agreed that the funds would be used for the Concert Hall's stage and acoustical sound reflectors, with an appropriate memorial plaque placed in the Concert Hall to designate the gift. On March 11, 1969, at the American Bandmasters Association Convention, it was announced that funds for the project had been raised through donations from 692 high school and community bands, as well as from individuals and businesses throughout the country.

Unfortunately, happy moments such as occurred while working for the Sousa memorial were not my typical experience in those days. The Watergate Town Development, as the adjacent project was called, gave us seemingly endless problems.

WATERGATE TOWN was being developed on approximately 10 acres, bounded by Virginia and New Hampshire avenues, F Street, and Rock

Creek Parkway. Occupied for almost a hundred years by the Washington Gas Light Company, the property was acquired in 1960 for $35 a square foot by a group of American and foreign investors headed by a subsidiary called Societa Generale Immobiliare (SGI), a publicly held Italian real estate company. Founded in 1862, SGI had 35,000 stockholders and assets in excess of $150 million. As a mark of further distinction, a substantial interest in it was held by the Vatican.

Although developers Royce Ward and Nicholas Salgo held the title in the name of Isle Vista, Inc., the project was commonly known as Watergate Town Development, or the Watergate Project. It took its name from the Watergate steps of the Memorial Bridge, where band concerts were held. Luigi Moretti, professor of architecture at the University of Rome, was the principal architect. Working with him was Milton Fisher, a member of the well-known Washington firm of Corning, Moore, Elmore, and Fisher, which specialized in the development of office and apartment building complexes.

Development of the site was authorized under the provisions of Article 75 of the D.C. zoning regulations. This article provided for the orderly development of tracts of land in excess of five acres and permitted "the design of a well-planned, large-scale residential development." An order granting the developers the right to proceed was issued on July 17, 1962, after public hearings the previous October. Considered to be an important part of the city's urban renewal program, the project promised to produce significant tax income to the District of Columbia, and local authorities were willing to cooperate with the developers in every way possible.

But as originally designed and sited, the Watergate complex raised real problems for the Center. One was its impact on the ingress and egress to the north side. On the developers' plans, F Street ran between the north side of the Center (see map, p.95) and what was to be the last building to be erected, identified as Building Number 1 of Stage IV. Besides the intolerable increase in traffic this building was sure to generate, its proximity threatened to overshadow the Center and virtually destroy "the parklike setting" that Congress had mandated. We were also worried about its proposed height, a worry that grew steadily worse as, for the better part of four years, the developers stubbornly declined to tell us precisely what they had in mind. When they finally unwrapped their plans for the Zoning Commission in 1967, we realized that our worst fears were justified: Building Number 1 was going to be 130 feet high. This was despite a ruling of the Fine Arts Commission that no building in the District could be higher than the Lincoln Memorial.

The developers were hardly ignorant of plans for a national cultural center on the Potomac when they acquired the Watergate property. In fact, as I said earlier, Moretti's design was based on Stone's first concept for the Center. Nor were they unaware of our objections, which we and the NCPC had voiced as early as September 1962. Indeed, the Fine Arts Commission had expressed its concern even earlier when, in a statement to the Zoning Commission the previous April, it said:

> The commission is concerned about the density of the Watergate development. We believe the "maximum park character" should be preserved in any new project in this area. The Commission does not agree with the [developers'] architect's contention that the open park-like character of adjoining lands has been extended into the site plan of the building project.

Stevens and the board authorized me to take every step possible to oppose construction of Building Number 1 as planned. For the next six years, taking every legal recourse I could think of, I fought the issuance of a building permit. I even went so far as to discuss the matter with the assistant attorney general, Edwin Weisl, Jr. He agreed to bring an injunction proceeding against the Watergate developers and representatives of SGI if a permit were to be issued. I also went to work drafting a complaint, meaning to have it ready should the Zoning Commission grant the permit, as I more than half expected it to do.

Hoping to solve the problem amicably, Stevens and I met frequently with representatives of SGI and the Vatican's counsel, both in D.C. and in New York. To no avail. The developers would not agree to shift the location of Building Number 1. Nor would they entertain any suggestion that they reduce the floor area; in fact, at one time they sought approval to increase the square footage to 719,420, an amount considerably over the total authorized for high-rises. They also argued that, properly, they shouldn't even be talking with us because, in their view, we had no authority. The land, they said, did not belong to the Center but to the U.S. government. At some point, the Watergate property was conveyed to the John Hancock Mutual Life Insurance Company as part of a financing plan under which Hancock took an equity interest. The change, however, had no effect on the position of the developers. They remained inflexible.

As far as we were concerned, the crux of the legal issue was embodied in Section (d) of the same order—issued July 17, 1962, by the Zoning Commission—that had authorized development of the Watergate Project. It provided that

> the height of the section or building designated as Number 1 shall be subject to possible adjustment, the extent and location of which shall be discussed with the Board of Zoning Adjustment. The Board, however, before authorizing such adjustment shall ascertain the views and opinions of the National Capital Planning Commission, the Commission of Fine Arts, the Commissioners of D.C. and the Director of the National Park Service, following which (the Board) shall make these . . . opinions known to the Zoning Commission.

In June 1967, nearing the construction date for Building Number 1, the Watergate developers realized they had to obtain official clarification of Section (d) and approval of a definite height, which they were now procedurally required to disclose. So, initiating an appeal, they filed two alternative sets of plans with the Zoning Commission. The plans were then forwarded to the Board of Zoning Adjustment, and from the BZA to the four agencies for comment. From then on it was a battle royal.

It was our contention that the BZA had no authority to set height over the 90-foot limit allowable under zoning regulations; it could vary that limit by only 5 percent pursuant to Section 7501.72. In any event, we said, Building Number 1 would have to be lower than the cornice of 110 feet of the Kennedy Center, a height approved by the NCPC, under whose jurisdiction the Center fell. I said as much in a brief to the BZA and addressed the issue again in a statement prepared for Stevens to deliver to the Fine Arts Commission on September 20.*

---

* Protests of this sort, voiced regularly while we waited for the commission to act, inspired a tart editorial in the *Washington Post* on October 13. It criticized the Center's trustees for their "unattractive arrogance—as though their project had a life of its own apart from the life of the city it is to serve—in asking that the completion of the Watergate suddenly be forbidden now that it is almost two-thirds built."

A week later, on September 27, the opinions of the review agencies were presented to the Zoning Commission. Of the four, the NCPC spoke most directly and encouragingly to our concern. It recommended that a decision on the developers' plans be delayed for a period "not to exceed three months" so that a study could be made of the relationship of Building Number 1 to the Kennedy Center. Thereupon the commission directed the BZA to take no action until the NCPC reported back to the commission at its first executive meeting in January 1968.

Meanwhile, the Watergate developers had completed Stages I and II and were in the midst of Stage III. It was self-evident that they had to have a decision on the 1962 order, and they were getting nervous. Arthur Hatton, secretary of the Zoning Commission, was holding up issuance of a building permit pending the NCPC report, and the developers had good reason to believe that one might never be forthcoming unless they made significant changes in the design and siting of the building. Even if they were not aware of the Department of Justice's intention to file for an injunction, they most certainly knew that we were ready to file a complaint should a permit be granted.

By now they were as tired of the delays as we were, and it was clearly in our mutual interest to come to an agreement. This we did, with the help of the NCPC and their designers, the Center's architect, the NPS, and perhaps most of all, Secretary of Interior Stewart Udall and an assistant, Henry L. Kimmelman. After a series of delicate and tense discussions, the developers agreed to split Building Number 1 in half and to rotate it 180 degrees. In accordance with recommendations from Stone and the NCPC, the top-floor level was reduced to 110 feet, and the building was repositioned toward New Hampshire Avenue, thereby opening up an area of 350 additional feet between it and the Center. This rotation had the effect of making the Center the visually dominant edifice with an opened-up park vista. It met the Center's aesthetic objections to the construction as previously planned and also provided better ingress and egress on the north side of the Center's parking garage. The NPS agreed to give access to the parkway from the Watergate garage; Watergate agreed to allow Center patrons to use its parking facilities whenever the Center's own garages were full. In addition, Watergate got a zoning modification so that Building

Number 1 was no longer restricted to residential use and could be opened to the offices and embassies that occupy it today.

The settlement obviated the need for litigation on the very eve of it. Our agreement was quickly processed through the Zoning Commission, the developers got their permit, and seven years of adversarial proceedings were over.*

All the while, our contractor had been moving along with construction of the Center itself. On January 29, 1967, a "topping-out" ceremony had been held on that part of the Center known as the Concert Hall, during which an 11-foot steel replica of a cello, courtesy of Bethlehem Steel, was hoisted to the roof. On September 3, 1969, another ceremony was held, this time to top out the Eisenhower Theater although it would not be officially named that until a month later. Again thanks to Bethlehem Steel, giant replicas of the Greek masks of comedy and tragedy were hoisted 109 feet and placed on the topmost steel girder. The workers celebrated with a beer party.

Progress was being made, and it was there for everybody to see. Pessimism and controversy were stilled. There was no more bitterness over the site. What the public might once have thought to be pie-in-the-sky was in the fall of 1970 visible and real.

From the moment of his appointment by President Kennedy, Stevens had performed unfailingly in character—gutsy, optimistic, always tenacious, and usually implacable. Now he, and all of us who had come to share his vision, had the satisfaction of knowing that a promised miracle on the Potomac was about to be achieved.

---

* Throughout these negotiations we had the counsel of Norman Glasgow, a partner in Wilkes and Artis and an expert in zoning law. He helped in many ways behind the scenes, and his public service should be a matter of record.

8

CRISIS:
We Face Work Stoppages, Deficits, and Vandalism

*T*he Center was a unique and complex project. We knew that from having read the plans. But it was only after we came to face the infinite details and interlocking problems of construction that we began to appreciate what it meant to be engaged in a venture of such unprecedented scale and intricacy.

Notwithstanding the first federal appropriations in 1964 and the success of our first campaign to raise private funds, we were always short of money. Construction costs escalated at a startling rate during the Vietnam War years. It was a problem that became seriously compounded when, as explained earlier, the bids came in and we learned that GSA and the architect had underestimated the amount of steel needed.

To avoid delays and further mistakes, Roger Stevens and the board set up as many safeguards as one could contemplate. We hired a watchdog—Col. William Powers, who had supervised construction of New York's Lincoln Center—and made him executive director for engineering. And GSA set up a project review committee, made up of Center officials, various GSA experts, the architect, the general contractor, and members of the board's Building Committee. Its purpose was to make sure that funds were available before we entered into a contract and that construction proceeded with as few surprises as possible. Gloomily, this group looked at the progress reports and contemplated the revised cost estimates, which, as of March 30, 1969, had climbed to $52 million. Their conclusion was inevitable. The Center needed more money. Help would have to come from Congress.

We decided at a board meeting that we should approach Congress for $12.5 million and so advised the contractors and major subcontractors. This was a difficult proposition because, for one reason or another, the Center had many enemies on the Hill, particularly on the House side. Orchestrating the approach to Congress was to be my job.

I first discussed the request with Dick Sullivan, by now an old friend. I also approached Kenneth Gray (D-Ill.), the eloquent chairman of the Public Buildings and Grounds Subcommittee of the House Public Works Committee. Like Sullivan, he was also receptive to the request. I then touched base with Rep. William H. Harsha (R-Ohio), who served on the Public Works Committee from 1961 to 1980 and was the ranking Republican on Gray's subcommittee. Harsha had long been a friend in court and a stalwart supporter of the Center, toiling diligently to ameliorate the minority of Republican opposition to it. He worked with Bob Jones and later Ken Gray on both sides of the aisle, effectively wielding a great deal of power. His influence was evident in every legislative step of the way for 18 years.

After these discussions, the House Public Works Committee informally agreed to enlarge the Center's borrowing authority by $5 million and to increase matching appropriations by $7.5 million to avoid a work stoppage. To cover all bases, I also met with members and staff of the Senate Public Works Committee and with the Appropriations committees of both the House and the Senate.

On May 14, 1969, Ken Gray introduced H.R. 11249 to amend the John F. Kennedy Center Act to authorize additional funds. This would increase appropriations to $23 million, to be matched by private funds, and increase borrowing authority from the Treasury to $20.4 million. The House Public Works Committee scheduled hearings for May 29, at which Bill Schmidt, commissioner of Public Buildings for GSA, Chairman Stevens, and I testified as a trio.

Schmidt, speaking as the Center's agent for design and construction, made an extended, candid statement to justify the need for additional funding. He based his presentation on the estimated gross cost at the time of $66.2 million, which was almost $20 million above the January 1964 estimate. In partial explanation, he pointed out that 30 percent of the increase was attributable both to errors in specifications by GSA and the architect and to changes in program requirements after work had started. "Thus," he summarized, "up to $14 million could be charged to cost of escalation."

Since some of the work had already been done, a conservative estimate of cost escalation was $9 million. Some of that escalation was due to events beyond our control, including a strike of the longshoremen, which prevented timely receipt of marble from Italy. Also unanticipated were the increased costs amounting to $0.6 million for glazing and insulation of the Center to ensure jet noise "attenuation." Another $1.2 million was due to change orders, a fairly common occurrence in a large and complex project. Schmidt pointed out that the rest of the increase was due to underestimation of the costs of structural steel and concrete form work. He added that

> tonnage of estimated steel was underestimated by about one-third. . . . In other words, GSA had estimated 12,800 tons of steel, the architect-engineer estimated 12,400 tons, and the proposal submitted was from 17,100 to 17,500 tons, at least a 33 percent increase in estimated steel tonnage and a unit cost increase of $60 per ton, . . . going from $390 per ton in the estimate to $450 in the low bid.

As the project went along, the estimates were being revised upwardly. By the end of 1967, the total estimated cost was $60.3 million; by the end of 1968, $61.9 million; and on March 31, 1969, $66.2 million. Schmidt made it clear that "without the additional funds the Center cannot be completed."

Not surprisingly, committee members were critical of Stone for underestimating the cost of the steel required by $2.7 million. Some congressmen felt he bore some responsibility and wanted GSA to investigate whether the $2.7 million differential could be recovered from the architect. Despite these criticisms, we had strong supporters. Texas congressman James Wright, a member of the board of trustees, backed our request warmly, saying

> I am going to support the bill, to do the best I can to help justify the bill, for the very plain and simple reason that I do not want

to see the project uncompleted. We have committed ourselves to the idea of constructing this memorial to the late President Kennedy, having a useful cultural adjunct to the city of Washington.

While most of the committee seemed to agree, they wanted assurances. We were asked whether we expected to come back for still more money. Stevens said it was "the duty of the trustees to complete the building," but, again, the committee pressed us to pledge not to return for additional funding. Fortunately, we were able to get away with a promise to do the best we could, so long as circumstances did not change drastically.

On June 12, 1969, the committee filed its report on H.R. 11249 and recommended passage, finding that the increase could be charged to escalation of construction costs. It rejected the idea of delaying some work to a later date. Such a course of action seemed impractical, and estimates were that a delay would probably result in an additional $10 million in costs. The committee made it clear, however, that under no circumstances would it consider a request for additional funds for construction.

On July 8, 1969, the full House turned to the proposal. Rep. Thomas P. ("Tip") O'Neill, Jr. (D-Mass.) called for debate on the House Rules Committee resolution; if this resolution did not pass the Rules Committee, the bill could never come to the floor for a vote. The resolution was bitterly opposed. Long-time critic Gross referred to it as a "real boondoggle." Frank Bow of Ohio, the ranking Republican on the House Public Works Committee and a member of the Board of Regents of the Smithsonian, called it a "national disgrace" and a "beautiful morgue." He was so exercised that a few minutes after his tirade he collapsed on the floor of the House and had to be hospitalized for a few days.

Despite the passion of the opposition, when put to a vote the resolution passed 75 to 47. This cleared the way for debate on the bill itself.

Representative Gray led off with a spirited 30-minute defense of the proposal. He stressed that matching funds on a 50-50 basis was a good idea, something that perhaps could be applied to other facilities, such as the new buildings for the FBI and the Department of Labor. He emphasized that the $66 million structure, although a fitting monument to the late president, was not being built for the Kennedys. It was for the American people, a place for artists to display their talents. He added,

> We ought to be proud here today of the great Center being built on the banks of the Potomac River. We ought to be here approving a partnership of a nation where people are willing to dig into their pockets to the tune of $24 million to provide a facility for all Americans.

Gray went on to say,

> The Cultural Center on the shores of the Potomac is now 50 percent finished and if this building is to be completed, we must have this legislation. It is that simple.

The debate was not without its caustic moments. Gross said he was surprised that Aristotle Onassis, the new husband of Jacqueline Kennedy, was not giving some of his money to the Center. Nevertheless, he said he would vote for the House appropriation since the project was so far along.

House Minority Leader Gerald Ford (R-Mich.) spoke to the issue of inaccurate estimates. He said GSA (which oversees all federal buildings) was investigating possible action against the Center's architect for miscalculating the cost of steel, "a $2.7 million error." Some congressmen argued that we had given our word that the building would never cost more than the original $15.5 million appropriated. Others argued that President Kennedy already had monuments in his honor. Our congressional advocates, however, concentrated on the practicalities. To delay would put the Center in the same position as the Washington Monument, which was left unfinished for 22 years, from 1854 to 1876, because Congress would not come up with the necessary money. They also maintained that it would be a national disgrace if the Center were left unfinished. Gray expounded on Eisenhower's contribution in signing the original legislation and on the bipartisan support that the Center had enjoyed from its inception.

A quorum was called and a vote taken on a motion to recommit. The motion was defeated: 162 yeas, 217 nays, and 53 abstentions. We began to breathe easier. A vote was then taken on H.R. 11249. It passed, 210 to 162.

We next turned to the Senate, and there we were in for some surprises. In testimony before the Senate Subcommittee on Public Works on July 14, 1969, first Representative Gray and then Stevens repeated the arguments they had given previously to the House Public Works Committee. Robert B. Foster, Jr., deputy to Bill Schmidt of GSA, followed. Happily, it was a short meeting before a friendly committee. On July 23, 1969, the full committee approved the House-passed authorization bill.

The matter was to be brought up on the Senate floor on September 24. Full debate was delayed, however, because, to our dismay, Sen. Margaret Chase Smith (R-Me.) introduced an amendment to H.R. 11249 requiring a GAO report before additional funds could be authorized. She also requested a full-fledged hearing like the one held the week before to investigate charges of overruns on the C5A aircraft.

We were surprised by her amendment because we did not see the two situations as analogous. Since Senator Smith was a friend,* I approached her off the Senate floor and also spoke to her administrative aide, offering any material she required to substantiate our need for more money. Unmoved, she insisted on the investigation. Her reputation was such that Majority Leader Mike Mansfield, always a friend to the Center, acceded to her request. Other powerful senators such as Harry K. Byrd, Jr. (D-Va.), John J. Williams (R-Del.), and Barry Goldwater (R-Ariz.) also supported her.

This turn of events caused tremendous consternation and unhappiness. Bear in mind, the Center was in dire need of funds. Certain subcontracts were being held up, and the fear was spreading among the crews that the Center would indeed be a "white elephant." For congressional action to be stalled now, pending an inquiry that could only confirm the facts as we had already presented them, was enough to endanger further construction. We felt powerless. Then in another surprising turn, Sen. Jennings Randolph, chairman of the Public Works Committee, saved the day. He advised that he had already requested a report from GAO and that it was expected momentarily. Our bill was kept on track.

The GAO report was actually delivered on October 6, serving to heighten interest in the Senate floor debate, which opened that same day.

* In 1951 I had represented the Republican minority as assistant counsel to the Senate Election and Privileges Committee, of which Margaret Chase Smith was a member, in the Maryland U.S. Senate election contest between Joseph Tydings and John Marshall Butler.

Senators Fulbright and Claiborne Pell (D-R.I.) spoke on our behalf, but from the response it was clear that even our friends in the Senate did not want to see us return to Congress for more funds in the future. Sen. Charles H. Percy (R-Ill.) spoke very personally to this point, saying "I am, without any equivocation or qualification, committing myself, as a trustee, to resign before we will come back to Congress for funds to finish this building."

Efforts of Senators Randolph and Mansfield helped push the matter through, and it was brought to a vote this same day. Just as we'd anticipated, the GAO report substantiated our testimony, and Senator Smith's amendment was defeated by a vote of 47-21, with 32 senators abstaining. The bill itself then passed 62-3, with 35 senators abstaining. It was especially satisfying to see Senators Goldwater and Williams among those in favor.

P.L. 91-90 was signed by President Nixon on October 17, 1969. It granted the Center borrowing authority and a provision for matching funds. But before these additional funds could be assured, legislation was necessary from the Appropriations committees of both houses. Thus, over the next three months, Stevens and I made the rounds with Foster of GSA, testifying in turn as hearings were called by three different subcommittees. Finally, on December 11, a supplemental appropriation for the 1970 fiscal year was passed by a voice vote in the House. Senate approval followed a week later, and on the day after Christmas, P.L. 91-166 was signed. We now had the prospect of $7.5 in matching funds. Now all we had to do was raise another $7.5 million from private sources.

WHILE WE WERE HAPPY to have the matter resolved, the delay had proved costly. Parliamentary tactics had slowed us down every step of the way. Although funds were authorized, the Appropriations committees had a lawful obligation to review the legislation and even a right to reject an appropriation. It took from May until December, almost seven months, to obtain final approval from Congress.

Nevertheless, we had much to be pleased about. Between 1967 and 1970 construction had moved along nicely. During 1967, we let the general contract along with 7 subcontracts, representing over $22 million in awards. One-third of the marble had already arrived from Italy, and 167 people were employed at the construction site. By December 1968, another 20 subcontracts had been let, amounting to nearly $9 million. At the end of 1968, the Center stood 25 percent complete, with the steel superstructure 92 percent finished.

Six months into 1969, the Center was half completed. Marble panels were in place on two exterior walls of the Concert Hall and along the Grand Foyer, completely enclosing the southernmost third of the building. During the previous 12 months, five subcontracts were let, representing $4 million in awards. In early March of 1970 the last piece of marble was placed in the exterior wall; the building was now fully enclosed. By June 30 the Center stood 75 percent complete, and 600 construction workers were on the job. Six additional subcontracts were let during 1970 at a cost of $1.6 million, bringing to 38 the total number of competitive awards made since construction began in 1965. There was reason to believe we would be able to open officially in 1971. Optimism ran high.

I must admit, though, that some days my optimism turned to pessimism. Rising costs for materials and labor were reaching the point of no control, and the general contractor and major subcontractors were grumbling. While they acknowledged that some of the unexpected increases could be attributed to the extraordinary inflation of the Vietnam War era, they also blamed us and GSA. In particular, they cited delays resulting from excessive design changes, which, in turn, had introduced problems of government supervision and created further delays getting their work approved for payment. All this, inevitably, resulted in claims against GSA and the Center for delay damages, which the contractors were having trouble collecting. On September 3, 1969, Pierce Associates, the mechanical contractor, took action. In a letter to the board of trustees, it asserted its right to damages and gave notice of its intention to terminate work within 30 days.

On October 13, with winter approaching and work in place endangered by lack of heat, this subcontractor withdrew its work force, claiming that the government had breached its contract. Fortunately, strenuous negotiations produced an interim agreement, and the Pierce crews returned to work on November 12. The crisis was by no means over, however. While negotiations toward a final settlement continued, GSA set up a task force to sort out the damages—in particular, to determine the extent to which Stone, the architect/engineer, might be liable for faulty contract documents. Moreover, the Pierce action moved a number of other subcontractors to assert similar claims through the prime contractor, John McShain.

These disputes, accompanied as they were by the long and unnerving process of getting the special appropriation through Congress, created great anxiety. Although delay claims clearly had to be paid to the extent they were meritorious, the Center had no funds available, and very much on the minds of the trustees was the warning from Congress not to return for more money.

By the fall of 1970 the claims were still unsettled. In protest, Ernst-Fischbach pulled its employees off the site on October 1, and a week later Pierce Associates again followed suit. Just as the weather was turning cold, all electrical, heating, air conditioning, plumbing, and other mechanical work ceased. The situation was critical, even more so than it was the previous fall. If some accommodation could not be reached, the job would be completely shut down and the Center would be without heat during the winter months. A shutdown, we feared, would result in irreparable damage to work already in place, compelling us to close the Center and put it in "mothballs." Quite simply, this could have ruined the project.

The trustees decided that the Center should take extraordinary steps to get work resumed, at least until the building was heated, but we soon learned that there was no possible way to work out any sort of arrangement through GSA. Therefore, I conferred with the comptroller general, Elmer Staats, and his counsel, Paul Dembling. I obtained from them oral authorization for the trustees to conclude a separate agreement with John McShain, whereby the electrical and mechanical subcontractors would receive from the Center's donated trust funds, dedicated for public purposes, some advances against their claims.

Our Building Committee hoped this interim arrangement would give GSA sufficient time to process the delay claims and to negotiate GAO approval of a settlement offer. With this course in mind, we began exhaustive negotiations with McShain, reaching a consensus on October 17. Two days later we had worked out an agreement under which the two subcontractors would return to work in full force. The agreement, though, was good for only 90 days; the expiration date was January 20, 1971. As it turned out, the electrical contractor did not return to work until November 1, and the mechanical contractor didn't put his men back on the site until November 19. With the calendar staring us in the face, GSA staffers and members of its various study groups, which with me constituted a frayed but very determined negotiation team, worked around the clock. None of us got much sleep.

In the previous July, Stevens had suffered a mild heart attack, a circumstance that added to our general anxiety and might have distracted us even more if it had not been for Robert O. Anderson, our vice chairman. One of the nation's leading industrialists, Anderson was at the time president and chief operating officer of the Atlantic Richfield Oil Company. During this crisis he was unfailingly responsive and competent, finding time, through correspondence and telephone conversations, to give the Center daily attention while continuing to manage the affairs of his business.

On November 10, at a special meeting of the board conducted by Anderson, we took up three reports regarding the status of construction, limitation of funds, and the agreements reached with McShain. In Anderson's judgment our resolution of the disputes was as satisfactory as anyone could reasonably expect.

At this meeting we also took up the product of the so-called Gertzensang-Lund Report, one of the several studies commissioned by GSA. In it, GSA maintained not only that the delay claims were heavily inflated but also that there were counterclaims to be asserted, especially against Stone. Irrefutably, underestimation by the architect/engineer had caused initial delay, and this liability was being reviewed by the Department of Justice, which represented us.

At this same meeting, the board moved to defer more than $1,873,000 in items until funding could be found to cover them.

Our situation was grim. Funds in hand and those anticipated included $3.5 million from APCOA under its parking concession agreement. Available, but not readily, was a combination of private gifts and federal matching funds amounting to an additional $3 million, including $1.5 million in fresh money. Against this, we faced mounting construction costs, which Colonel Powers,* after reviewing anticipated expenditures through completion, put at $70,685,000, including an estimated $3.3 million in delay damages. His estimate was considerably more than the total of funds already expended and those immediately available to us.

In the event that settlements were not reached with the electrical and mechanical subcontractors before their work extension agreements expired, they could either (1) continue to work and sue for damages or (2) walk off the job, which would require the trustees to bring in new subcontractors.

Notwithstanding the uncertainties and problems, the trustees wanted to open the building no later than September 1971. During Stevens's recovery I was allowed to visit him briefly in New York, where I updated him on construction progress. To expedite matters, especially in regard to the claims, Stevens recommended that special counsel be retained to review the delay damage claims of Pierce and Ernst-Fischbach and Moore, Inc. In effect, he wanted to obtain a second opinion on GSA's Gertzensang-Lund Report.

Stevens returned to his duties once his doctors gave him a clean bill of health, and on January 22, 1971, he presided over his first board meeting since his illness. We were pleased to see him back in charge, and it was to the future that we turned. The trustees gave him authority to execute contracts for educational and performing arts programs and for the operation of the Center, with a restraining promise that any commitment of more than $50,000 required prior approval by the Executive Committee. It was the consensus of the board that the chairman might wish to define further the procedures for scheduling and contracting, and that he should do so in consultation with the Executive Committee.

Prior to that, however, at a meeting of the Executive Committee on December 3, Stevens was authorized to engage the services of special counsel from the law firm of Covington and Burling. Senior partner Alfred Moses and William Livingston of that firm assumed responsibility to

---

* When Colonel Powers terminated his employment with the Center in early 1970, his place was filled on a part-time basis by Bill Schmidt, who was no longer commissioner of Public Buildings for GSA. Schmidt's reputation for independence of judgment and integrity was impeccable. He was a top government official and had the respect and confidence of GSA, the Office of Management and Budget (OMB), the Treasury, and Congress.

resolve the delay damage claims of the two subcontractors. Sometime later, having sifted out the many complexities, they reported that the Center would have to pay some damages. In its internal report, GSA agreed.

Our original agreements with McShain and with Ernst-Fischbach and Pierce Associates had set a deadline of January 19, 1969, for the completion of construction. It looked now as if their work would not be finished until June 30, 1971. This delay of 30 months was at the heart of the problem. In its report to the Center, the GSA task force concluded that 18 of these 30 months were attributable to government causes. I demurred. In a memorandum to GSA, I called their conclusions and analyses erroneous. The task force had looked at government records only; it had not reviewed the files of the general contractor or those of the two subcontractors, nor had it interviewed other important subcontractors such as Bethlehem Steel.

Negotiations over delay damage claims continued for several years. Litigation followed in both the Court of Claims and U.S. District Court for the District of Columbia when Pierce sued the trustees on the 1970 agreement. Once suit was filed, the Department of Justice took over the responsibility for defending us against the claims of the general contractor, the subcontractors, and the architect, and for prosecuting our counterclaims against them. The department was represented by William D. Ruckelshaus, deputy attorney general; Irving Jaffe, assistant attorney general, Civil Division; and Jaffe's associate, Frances Nunn. Kenneth Parkinson, counsel for general contractor McShain, vigorously protected his client's interests.

Meanwhile, the Center explored every avenue to cut and defer. GAO allowed us to use trust funds for the settlement of claims, including advances on those for delay damages. Every type of payment was used to keep construction on schedule and to get the Center operational by September 1971. It was a long and complex process.

We did open in 1971 according to plan. It was not, however, until October 18, 1974, that the first judgment settling a portion of the cases was entered in the Court of Claims. The judgment was against the United States of America and in favor of McShain for $485,958.80.

The procedural steps necessary to obtain payment of such a damage judgment from the United States entail a special supplemental appropriation from Congress. Funds generally are appropriated as a matter of course.

The course, however, can be long and tedious, and Pierce Associates was adamant about payment. Contending that contractually it was due to have been paid by October 25, 1974, the company filed for summary judgment in the District Court. Unfortunately, it was not within our power to determine when Congress would provide supplemental appropriation funds. Actually, deficiency judgments and other judgments are covered in supplemental appropriations twice a year, once in the spring and once in the fall. So neither McShain nor Justice had any control over payment of the claims. They would be paid in due course. On October 25, the Justice Department advised Treasury by letter that the Court of Claims judgment could be certified to Congress. Congress considered it as part of the spring supplemental appropriations bill. Eventually, the bill was signed by President Ford on June 12, 1975, and on June 23 the U.S. Treasury drew a check to McShain. The Kennedy Center remitted a separate amount as part of a settlement agreement. U.S. District Court Judge Oliver Gasch denied further motions, and on July 25 he dismissed the case involving Pierce. The remainder of the litigation continued for some years until it was settled in similar fashion with payment of judgments by the United States.*

This was a busy time for me and my son, William W. Becker, who was practicing law with me. During the critical periods of the construction claims, delay damage claims, and actions of the creditors, we worked steadily with government officials, including those from Justice, Interior, OMB, GSA, and members of Congress and their staffs. To our great relief, we were able to conclude the history of construction with little fanfare compared with how that history began.

WHILE WE WERE STILL COPING with the claims problems, we began to confront the issue of how the Center's operation and maintenance were to be funded. At the time—in late 1970—it looked as if the Center might be burdened with all expenses, including those related to accommodation of millions of tourists. Clearly, these expenses were far beyond the capacity

---

* McShain brought suit against the trustees in the Court of Claims for $1,364,000, the construction costs, and for $12,000, the balance of the contractor's fees. This suit, like the others, was settled by the Justice Department.

of any conventional theatrical organization to meet from ticket sales or private contributions.

The Center, of course, was never intended to be a conventional theater, or even a cluster of theaters. Nor was it an ordinary public institution. It was, rather, a distinctive public monument with two essential and different functions. One of its functions was to memorialize President Kennedy in the same way that other monuments memorialize Lincoln, Jefferson, and Washington. The other was to serve as a *living* memorial by providing facilities for the performing arts and nationwide educational programs. It seemed only proper, therefore, that some of the costs for maintenance and operation be assumed by the federal government. Stevens thought the time had come to take the matter to Congress, and with that prospect in mind the trustees authorized me to bring the subject up with the National Park Service.

The NPS, represented by Robert C. Horne, agreed it was fitting to develop a reasonable and fair formula of appropriations for that portion of the Center considered a memorial. On recommendation of James Bradley of the Smithsonian, we turned to Leonard Reamer of Fox and Co., a brilliant accountant who later died at an early age. He presented a formula agreeable to the NPS, the Center, and OMB. We then presented the proposals to Representative Gray, who subsequently worked them into a bill, H.R. 9801 (July 22, 1971).

I joined Stevens, Schmidt, and Reamer in testifying before the House Subcommittee on Public Buildings and Grounds. Also present for the hearing were William McCormick Blair, executive director of the Kennedy Center, and my son Bill. This was the first time Congress was faced with the question of how much the Center should pay for its performing arts share and how much the NPS should pay for monument costs. The bill, an amendment to the John F. Kennedy Center Act, authorized NPS funds for the support of nonperforming arts functions and for this purpose appropriated an initial sum of $1,500,000.

Schmidt's testimony was particularly important. It was based on his experience with other facilities and their operating staffs, and with U.S. Park Police and the Federal Protective Service on security requirements. He summed up the Center's needs as follows:

"For the People"

Every July 4 the public is invited (first come, first served) to watch fireworks from the terrace.

More than 115,000 young people attend Education Department performances each year. Here Chuck Davis welcomes schoolchildren to a free concert of African dance during an observance of Black History Month in the Laboratory Theater.

Trustee Jean Kennedy Smith, founder and chairman of Very Special Arts, with education director Jack Kukuk. Very Special Arts sponsors workshops for and performances by the disadvantaged.

Students from acting classes prepare for a production in the Theater Lab

Orval Hansen, chairman of the National Education Committee, with Burl Ives, AAE National Spokesperson for the Arts in Education.

Pupeteer Shari Lewis and young friend.

157

NSO Musical Director Rostropovich conducts a master class with Rachel Young, an NSO Youth Fellow.

The Australian play Summer of the Seventeenth Doll *was the entry of Hoftsra University (Hempstead, N.Y.) in the 11th annual American College Theater Festival, 1979. For several years the Festival was sponsored by the National Broadcasting Company.*

Sara Garcia as the grandmother and Martha Pearlman in the title role of Maggie Mogalita, *commissioned from Wendy Kesselman in 1984 and presented by Programs for Children and Youth in the Theater Lab.*

Celebrating Cultural Diversity . . .
The Shiloh Baptist Male Choir and Cathy Funk and Patsy Montana, performing at Third Annual Open House, 1987.

It is estimated that the total cost of operation, maintenance, and security during the first year will approximate $2,384,000. This covers the structure and its mechanical and electrical systems. This includes costs related to both performing arts and nonperforming arts activities, and the costs which are attributable primarily to performing arts activities which are to be financed from performance income.

Of this sum, $1,884,000 is applied to the nonperforming arts activities.

More generally, our testimony sought to make the point that we were dealing with a unique institution with two essential characteristics—one like that of other public monuments, the other peculiar to the Center's conception as a living memorial. Our case was well received, but legislation did not follow the usual process. As the summer wore on and as the building came to attract more and more tourists, we were stunned by an avalanche of incidents requiring increased security measures, the costs of which rapidly got out of hand. Our request for funds soon turned into a distress signal. Fortunately, the committee voted the $1.5 million, and the bill went to the House with an assurance from Gray that "this is the last time we'll have to bail out the JFK Center." It was a statement he later had cause to regret.

The bill passed the House after floor debate and then proceeded to the House Committee on Appropriations, where extensive hearings were held under the chairmanship of Julia Butler Hansen (D-W.Va). Senators Percy and Fulbright introduced S. 2900, a legislative companion to the House measure, on November 23, 1971, and a few weeks later a hearing was held by the Subcommittee on Public Buildings and Grounds at which Percy gave some impressively convincing testimony. After approval by the committee, the bill passed the Senate, and in time the Committee on Supplemental Appropriations reported favorably on the $1.5 million appropriation.

The authorizing legislation was signed into law by President Nixon on June 16, 1972. As always, we were relieved, but also as always, we had to go through another anxious time—on this occasion almost six months—before the appropriations measure itself was passed. Fortunately, recognizing our need, Congress chose to direct the $1.5 million to the Center, rather than to the NPS, as reimbursement for the first year's operating costs and damages from vandalism.

In the next fiscal year a similar sum went to the Department of Interior for NPS to carry out its responsibilities. Under the law these include maintenance, security, information, and other services necessary to sustain the nonperforming arts functions. Sometime later a cooperative agreement was worked out, under which the NPS pays. 76.2 percent of the total costs for maintenance and operation and the Center 23.8 percent, this being the share attributable to performing arts activities. In 1989 these costs came to $4.5 million, of which the Center paid $1.2 million. The formula by which the shared costs are determined is essentially the same as the one Leonard Reamer worked out in 1971; it has withstood the test of time.

The assumption by the Park Service of responsibility for the Center's security was a critical matter for, to our consternation, beginning with the first stream of tourists, we had been hit by successive waves of vandalism. Apparently driven by some uncontrollable passion for souvenirs, visitors came with scissors and screwdrivers. They helped themselves to the crystal prisms on elevator chandeliers, a complete Waterford crystal wall sconce from the South Opera Lounge, marble handles from restroom faucets, and even toilet seats. Pieces of draperies and carpeting were cut, the scraps slipped into purses, taken home, and presumably pasted into family scrapbooks. Light switches were removed. Silverware and dishes from the restaurants were pilfered. People customarily identified on guest lists as VIPs somehow managed to take off with half the special tablecloths.

The defacement and destruction continued for at least a month after our dedication festivities in September. To stop it, the NPS had to station extra guards along the guided tour routes, at every point of entry, on the terrace, and in the theaters, restrooms, and restaurants. Before this astonishing epidemic of public larceny had run its course, the damages came to more than a million dollars. We had no choice but to close the building during nonperformance hours and to cancel the Christmas programs in the Grand Foyer. Many of the stolen items we found either impossible or unwise to replace.

Our public affairs director tried to explain the destructiveness as evidence of America's "love affair" with the Center. "People love it so much," he was quoted as saying, "that they are taking it with them, light bulb by light bulb."

Whatever it was—a love affair with the Center or, as one popular magazine suggested, "a compulsive desire for a link to the martyred president," or merely one of those mysterious self-limiting explosions of manic disorder that can turn a group into a mob—I leave to the social psychologists. It was clear, though, even before the opening night curtain, that the Center was affecting people as no other public monument had ever done.

9

CURTAIN UP:
The Center Today

*T*hough not widely recognized, it was a combination of the 1958 act to create a national cultural center and President Eisenhower's vigorous endorsement of the idea that made culture a legitimate concern of public policy in this country. Serial events in the center's development, beginning with the first congressional debates that defined its purpose, served to produce a climate more favorable to an appreciation of the arts than Washington, the city of politicians and bureaucrats, had ever known.* Indeed, what has become the Kennedy Center represents our government's most articulate commitment to "the Pursuit of Happiness"—perhaps the most revolutionary, certainly the most intangible, of the inalienable rights advanced in the Declaration of Independence.

Long before it opened its doors and even in its unfinished state, the Center was a favorite tourist attraction. To hometowns all over America the word went back that here on the Potomac was something worth waiting for. The opening itself was a national news story, so broadly anticipated that the *New York Times* gave it five columns on page one.

The Center formally opened with a two-day celebration on September 8 and 9, 1971.** The Opera House was dedicated on the first evening

---

* In 1964 Lyndon Johnson appointed the Center's chairman, Roger L. Stevens, as special assistant to the president. From that position Stevens spearheaded the campaign that led to creation of the National Council on the Arts, of which he was the first chairman, and subsequently to organization of the two national endowments for the arts and humanities.

** The first public use—a preview—of the Center occurred on May 17, 1971. On that evening, with President and Mrs. Nixon as patrons, a gala fund-raising event was held to benefit the Center's Educational Fund, which among other things would provide reduced-price tickets for students and senior citizens. About $250,000 was raised.

Opening night in the Opera House, September 8, 1971. Leonard Bernstein conducted the premiere performance of his Mass, *a Theatre Piece for Singers, Players, and Dancers, written in memory of President Kennedy. Alan Titus sang the role of celebrant, and among the other performers were Walter Williams, the Norman Scribner Choir, the Berkshire Boys' Choir, and the Alvin Ailey American Dance Theatre.*

with the premiere performancc of Leonard Bernstein's *Mass*, commissioned for the occasion at the request of Jacqueline Kennedy Onassis. Based on the liturgy of the Roman Mass and with additional text in English by Bernstein and Stephen Schwartz, the work was sung by Norman Scribner's Choir and by Alan Titus as the celebrant. It was conducted that night by the composer himself. The event was an appropriately impressive tribute to the assassinated president, although his widow was unable to attend.* Mrs. Rose Kennedy, arriving on the arm of her only surviving son, Sen. Edward Kennedy, was joined in the president's box by the senator's wife, Joan; Ethel Kennedy; Eunice Kennedy Shriver; other members of the Kennedy family; and Roger Stevens and his wife, Christine.

The Concert Hall opened the next night with a program by the National Symphony Orchestra, conducted by Antal Dorati, with violinist Isaac Stern as soloist. President and Mrs. Nixon were the honored guests. With them in the president's box or in adjoining boxes were their daughter Patricia and her husband, Edward Cox; Mrs. Mamie Eisenhower; Mrs. Rose Kennedy; the contralto Marian Anderson; Mr. and Mrs. David Lloyd Kreeger (he was then president of the National Symphony); Mr. and Mrs. Stevens;

---

* Mrs. Onassis came to the Center for the first time on June 5, 1972, the fourth anniversary of the assassination of Sen. Robert F. Kennedy, her brother-in-law.

Mrs. Joseph Kennedy arrives escorted by her son, Sen. Edward Kennedy. Out of courtesy to the Kennedy family, President Nixon did not appear at this first of the three opening nights.

Dedication of the Concert Hall, September 9, 1971. In the reception room of the president's box, the author and wife, Ann, follow Helen Hayes. With President Nixon are Mrs. Nixon and Mrs. Eisenhower.

and Mr. and Mrs. William Schuman. (Mr. Schuman's "Secular Cantata No. 2, A Free Song" was one of the evening's selections.) Also attending were members of the Kennedy family, members of the Nixon cabinet, and movie stars Gregory Peck and Charlton Heston.

The Eisenhower Theater was dedicated a month later, on October 18, in a fete chaired by Allie (Mrs. J. Willard) Marriott. The inaugural drama was *A Doll's House*, starring British actress Claire Bloom. President and Mrs. Nixon attended, as did Mr. and Mrs. John Eisenhower. Mrs. Dwight D. Eisenhower sent regrets; she was attending the dedication of the Eisenhower Museum in Abilene, Kan., and later the dedication of the Eisenhower Medical Center in Palm Springs, Calif.

Acoustics for the Center had been a matter of continuing concern. Although prior to the openings they had passed every test of technology and the human ear, it was nonetheless enormously reassuring to have them praised by first-night reviewers. On the morning after the National Symphony performance, Paul Hume of the *Washington Post* wrote:

> If the music lacks the kind of energy and thrust of the finest Beethoven, it gave the capacity audience an immediate demonstration of the magnificent quality of classical symphonic sound that Cyril Harris's flawless acoustics provide for the Concert Hall to match those of the Opera House.

Commenting especially on the quality of sound received in the balconies, Harold C. Schonberg of the *New York Times* said, "The Concert Hall may well be the finest acoustic installation in the country." He went

David Merrick's Mack and Mabel *(1976) brought the daughters of four recent presidents to the Center at the invitation of President and Mrs. Gerald R. Ford. From left: Margaret Truman Daniel, President Ford, Susan Ford, Linda Johnson Robb, Charles Robb, David Eisenhower, Julie Nixon Eisenhower, and Mrs. Ford.*

President Ford chats with Jacqueline Kennedy Onassis during intermission of Mack and Mabel.

on to describe the Opera House, without qualification, as "acoustically the finest."

From the moment it became fully operational, the Center has been open every day of the year. The first spring after its opening, tourists were showing up at the rate of 10,000 to 12,000 a day, making it second only to the Capitol in visitor traffic; at last count (spring 1989), it had attracted more than 50 million visitors from the United States and abroad. The Center has staged over 17,000 performances of more than 200 theatrical productions and presented more than 300 of the world's finest orchestras, dance troupes, opera companies, and chamber ensembles. All told, the performances have been attended by more than 21.5 million people. Extending far beyond the footlights, the Center has reached millions more through radio and television programs, touring productions, and education projects.

The record, I think, shows just how wrong some of the Center's early detractors were. It has not turned out to be the "monumental disaster" that Ada Louise Huxtable of the *New York Times* said it would be. Neither has it been the "white elephant" that Representative Widnall repeatedly called it, nor the "huge white whale washed ashore and grounded forever on the east banks of the Potomac," as the *Washington Monthly* once described it. Equally unfounded was Wolf von Eckardt's view that placing it on the Potomac "will lead us to commit a folly that would plague us for the next hundred years." No, indeed. What I believe is that the Center may in fact be leading us to "a golden renaissance" in the performing arts, which is what playwright Thornton Wilder once predicted.

From the beginning, the unique public-private partnership that built the Center and operates it today has been a strong energizing spirit. It must be remembered that the success of this entire multimillion-dollar project was always predicated on our ability to obtain private funding. This we did even though we had no reliable hard-core source of contributors, like a university with a body of loyal alumni, and we had to work under severe congressional pressure to meet goals with statutory deadlines. For this reason, the Center has a history and a constituency that makes it significantly different from a similar center in Ottawa, which was built and has all its operations paid for by the Canadian government. Nor can it be compared with London's government-funded, government-administered theater complex on the Thames.

We have had only two disappointments worth noting. The first was the outbreak of contagious larceny described in chapter 8, which blessedly was short-lived. Our second came some five years later when water from a few hundred leaks ruined the plaster, carpets, walls, and wallscapes in the Grand Foyer and other areas. The leaks occurred in the roof, roof terraces, and ceilings, and the water streamed down through more leaks in the kitchen floors of the restaurants. We were forced to close the restaurants for six months, and once again it was necessary to put the Grand Foyer off limits. But by rerouting patrons through the back and side doors and building plywood walkways over the wet floors, we were able to keep to the performance schedule without interruption. This time, the estimated cost was $4.5 million. The last thing in the world we wanted to do was to go back to Congress for more money, but there was nothing in the budget to cover such a disaster, so back we went. Fortunately, Rep. Ken Gray, always a good and stalwart friend, took our request and succeeded in overcoming the objections of his colleagues. Six months later, in late June of 1977, Congress appropriated the $4.5 million, and the NPS proceeded to repair the damage.

IN LARGE PART, the success of programming has been the result of early planning. As early as 1960, L. Corrin Strong had convinced the trustees of the importance of a well-rounded program. To help us plan, he retained Dr. Carlton Sprague Smith of the New York Public Library, a distinguished musical consultant. Smith submitted a comprehensive 77-page report aptly titled "What Goes Into It," based on the first architectural concept. The thrust of his recommendations was that the Center be structured as a creative force rather than as a rental operation—in other words, that it encourage the young and talented, and initiate the production of new works rather than merely book the proven and popular. To be sure, Smith's report was a bit premature since, in 1960, both critics and friends of the Center were almost entirely preoccupied with problems of design and location. His main point, however, was not lost on the trustees.

Early in 1965, Stevens, with the approval of the board, appointed a program committee under the leadership of Arthur M. Schlesinger, Jr. The committee consisted of Mrs. Thomas W. Braden, Center trustee; Harold Clurman, producer, director, and theater critic; Richard M. Goodwin, White House special assistant; August Heckscher, director of the Twentieth Century Fund and former White House consultant on the arts—the first ever to serve in that position; Goddard Lieberson, president of Columbia Records; Oliver Smith, New York theatrical designer; and George Stevens, Jr., director of the motion picture division of USIA. The committee also included Jacqueline Kennedy, Amb. Sol M. Linowitz, and Justice Abe Fortas. Heckscher's inclusion was important because of his influence on the arts in this country. He had prepared an extremely significant 80-page paper for President Kennedy entitled "The Arts and the National Government." In it he referred to the "growing awareness that the United States would be judged—and its place in history ultimately assessed—not by its military or economic power alone but by the quality of its civilization." I believe this report had a great influence on President Kennedy and subsequently on President Johnson.

The program committee met seven times in 1966 and, in its search for the most effective use of the Center's facilities, consulted regularly with outstanding professionals in the performing arts. Faithful to the congressional mandate, the committee studied theories and formats of arts management, the feasibility of resident companies, and the potential of public and commercial television to extend the range of activities. It recommended several changes in the original plan, all intended to make the

Center more flexible and to extend its educational area nationwide. By the time George London, the internationally famous opera star, arrived in the summer of 1968 to assume his duties as artistic director, all the important background studies were done.

During these years Stevens found frequent occasion to articulate his conviction that the Center would be

> a powerful and vital force that will influence, integrate, and invigorate the performing arts throughout the land, drawing the talents of the entire nation to this showplace on the Potomac.

He reiterated his desire for national companies of ballet, opera, and theater that "will seek to bring the genius of America's most promising talent directly to the entire nation."

Even so, some of our critics remained unconvinced. On June 10, 1969, Nicholas von Hoffman, a columnist writing in the *Washington Post*, took up the question of elitism, an issue somewhat related to programming. His brutal attack referred to

> rich guys in their dinner jackets and their superfluous wives—the same ladies who disport our women's pages from time to time— government biggies, chauffeurs, champagne, jewels, snobbery and knots of us peasants trying to guess the names of these important people.

Senator Fulbright introduced into the *Congressional Record* on July 11, 1969, Stevens's reply to von Hoffman's column. Stevens pointed out that on more than one occasion von Hoffman had been given the opportunity to familiarize himself with the programming plans, but for reasons of his own had shown no interest in ascertaining the facts. Had von Hoffman been listening, Stevens said, he would surely have known that the Center planned to present all types of music, for all kinds of audiences; George London, our artistic director, had repeatedly taken pains to say so publicly.

As a matter of policy, Stevens consistently associated the Center with celebrities who had reputations for popularizing the performing arts. Leonard Bernstein had played host to a series of television specials while retaining the respect of his peers as a composer and the musical director of the New York Philharmonic. Julius Rudel, director of the New York City Opera who served as our musical adviser from 1968 to 1975, was widely known for his ability to present opera at bargain prices.

That same year Stevens named the American Ballet Theatre the Center's resident ballet company, a position the ABT could not accept for economic reasons. The National Ballet of Washington, understandably disappointed not to have become the resident company, was invited to use the Center. The National Symphony, at first a tenant, is now the Center's affiliate, performing 28 weeks a year in the Concert Hall under the direction of Mstislav Rostropovich.

As completion neared, former critics began to change their minds, apparently in hopes of being a part of the Center's future. A good case in point was Patrick Hayes, Washington's leading impressario. In the early days Hayes had been a major and bitter adversary, helping organize the fight against the Potomac location and objecting repeatedly and loudly to the size of the facilities as planned. (Once when he and Sol Hurok complained that the Opera House was too small, Stevens told them, "We're building for the optimum of the artist and the public, and not for Mr. Hurok.") Hayes had won his reputation as the operator of the Friday Morning Music Club and the Hayes Concert Bureau. Looking ahead, in 1966 he organized the Washington Performing Arts Society (WPAS) with the idea that it would become an integral part of the Center's programming. Hayes had good professional ties to Hurok, Columbia Artists, and other big agents, and he convinced Stevens that he could provide capacity audiences. To his credit, he did develop WPAS into a prestigious and viable organization that has contributed importantly to the Center's mission.

Martin Feinstein, who was appointed executive director in January 1972, came to the Center after a distinguished career with the Hurok organization. For eight years he brought to the Opera House many of the world's great ballet and opera companies. He resigned in 1980 and for two years served as manager of the National Symphony, after which he became the general director of the Washington Opera. In his first decade there, the company experienced unprecedented growth, enjoying a vastly expanded financial base and an impressive increase in the number of its annual productions and performances. Although the company is not an integral part of the Center, it is in fact an associate organization that uses the Opera

House, the Eisenhower Theater, and the Terrace Theater. Its success has added luster to the Center's programming.

With Feinstein's departure, the position of executive director was abolished, Stevens himself assuming many of Feinstein's former duties. To pick up the functions of artistic director and to be responsible especially for the programming of dance, ballet, and opera, he turned to Marta Istomin, the widow of Pablo Casals and wife of the internationally known pianist Eugene Istomin. Working quietly and with great dignity, Mrs. Istomin has proved to be a skilled negotiator, bringing the best of the world's music, ballet, and opera to the Center's stages. To her everlasting credit, it was she who arranged to stage the Deutsche Oper Berlin's production of Wagner's *Ring des Nibelungen* in the Opera House the summer of 1989. Attesting the Center's arrival as a world-class theater, General-intendent Gotz Friedrich offered the presentation as an exclusive engagement in celebration of the 40th anniversary of the founding of the Federal Republic of Germany. Both cycles of the *Ring* were sold out, some Wagner devotees coming from as far as Australia to see it.

The Center honored composer Aaron Copland on his 80th birthday with a concert of his music conducted by Leonard Bernstein. The composer narrated his Lincoln Portrait.

Virtually every major American orchestra regularly appears at the Center: the Philadelphia Orchestra, the Cleveland Orchestra, the Chicago Symphony, the Detroit Symphony, the New York Philharmonic, the Los Angeles Philharmonic, the Boston Symphony Orchestra, and our own resident National Symphony. The Metropolitan Opera performed here until 1985, when escalating production and travel costs made Washington performances prohibitive. The New York City Opera, under Julius Rudel, performed for several seasons.

The Center has staged major festivals featuring the works of the great composers—Bach, Handel, Haydn, and Mozart. It has also become a showcase for outstanding chamber musicians in America, particularly during the summer Festival of Festivals and at Terrace Theater concerts throughout the year. The Kreeger String Series, funded by Washington philanthropist and cultural leader David Lloyd Kreeger and his wife, Carmen, is a popular annual event. The late Abe Fortas, more widely remembered as an associate justice of the U.S. Supreme Court but also an accomplished violinist and one of our distinguished musical trustees, is honored each year with a memorial concert; until his untimely death in 1982 he was a wise and helpful adviser to Stevens and me. Among other annual events are concerts by the Choral Arts Society, the Ontario Society, the Paul Hill Chorale, and the Kennedy Center Chamber Players.

What has become a triennial celebration at the Center began in May 1957 as National and Inter-American Music Week. The affair was high-lighted with a luncheon cosponsored by the Greater Washington Board of Trade, the Greater Washington Music Council, and the D.C. Recreation Department. At this luncheon, Marian Anderson was guest artist, Agnes Meyer the featured speaker, and I an active participant. Music was provided by the American Federation of Musicians Local through a grant from the Music Performance Trust Fund of the Recording Industries, thanks largely to the interest of Samuel Rosenbaum of Philadelphia, a fund trustee. A year later, this event was expanded into the Inter-American Music Festival under the auspices of the Organization of American States (OAS), of which Guillermo Espinosa was director of cultural affairs. Others active in the initial sponsorship were the Cultural Development Committee of the Board of Trade, of which I was chairman; Harold Spivacke, chief of the music division at the Library of Congress; Harold Boxer, director of music

A Kennedy Center gala brought together Yehudi Menuhin, Mstislav Rostropovich, Leonard Bernstein, and André Previn.

for the Voice of America; and Samuel Rosenbaum. For many years thereafter, the festival was held in various Washington auditoriums—Howard University, Lisner Auditorium of the George Washington University, Coolidge Auditorium at the Library of Congress, and Constitution Hall. Since 1971, however, most of its programs have been held in the Concert Hall. Individual artists and the works of major talents in Latin America have been featured at these festivals—for example, the Argentinean composer Alberto Ginestra, whose new opera, *Beatrix Cenci*, was one of the opening productions of the Opera House.

On May 21, 1974, a special two-day event was held to commemorate the 25th anniversary of the signing of the OAS charter. On the first day the festival orchestra was conducted by José Serbrier of Uruguay with violinist Jaime Laredo of Bolivia. The 96-year-old Pablo Casals was scheduled to conduct on the second day; when his health kept him off the podium, however, Alexander Schneider stepped in and led the orchestra through a number of Casals's compositions. Also appearing that day, to equally great acclaim, was the Choral Arts Society of Washington under the direction of Norman Scribner. Four years later, the festival honored Villa Lobos, the great Brazilian composer, conductor, and artist, on the 90th anniversary of his birth. The entire program consisted of Lobos compositions, and his widow was the guest of honor.

Since 1977 Harold Boxer has continued as an exemplary director of the festival, now known as the Inter-American Music *and Arts* Festival. The 1988 Film Festival of the Americas was mostly his inspiration.

The Center has sponsored a number of musical competitions over the years, and through them has actively assisted aspiring artists as well as established recitalists. Chief among these competitions are the annual Friedheim Awards for the composition of American works in symphonic or chamber music. In 1985, entries were received from 200 composers.

The Center regularly books international stars, many of whom have never before performed for American audiences. Prominent among these presentations have been appearances by Italy's Teatro alla Scala, the Peking Opera, and other opera companies from Paris and Vienna. The Center has offered the Stuttgart, Royal London, Royal Danish, and Bolshoi ballets, and the Berlin, Vienna, London, Leningrad, and Concertgebow of Amsterdam orchestras. Foreign artists—Jean-Pierre Rampal, Carlos Montoya, Andrés Segovia, Luciano Pavarotti, Placido Domingo, Joan Sutherland, Pinchas Zukerman—have come to recognize the Kennedy Center as the most prestigious stage in America.

That film is established as one of the performing arts at the Center is to the credit of Richard Coe, drama critic for the *Washington Post.* In a piece published on June 9, 1962, he regretted that no accommodation was made in our plans for the study, viewing, and preservation of the motion picture. It was a point well taken by Roger Stevens, who subsequently met in Coe's office with George Stevens, Jr. (no relation), then chief of the USIA film division, to explore possibilities. Immediately the perennial questions arose: Assuming space could be found, how should a film program be structured and where would the money come from?

When Stevens became chairman of the National Council on the Arts in 1965, he turned the questions over to the Stanford Research Institute. With the Stanford report in hand, he then got three grants—one from the NCA, one from the Ford Foundation, and one from seven members of the Motion Picture Association. Each was for $1,100,000. With George Stevens as director, the American Film Institute was launched in 1967, and AFI became the Center's "official resident film company." The problem then became one of getting the motion picture industry to give money. Finally, after a generous gift from Jack Warner, a 224-seat theater was built, fitted into unused space backstage of the Eisenhower Theater.

The AFI has since shown an average of 700 films a year, everything from film classics of the past to experimental movies by today's most talented young directors. With administrative offices at the Center, AFI has ties to the industry in Hollywood and around the world. It carries on an energetic research program and, in cooperation with the Library of Congress, conducts a program to retrieve, conserve, and reproduce important films that might otherwise be lost.

THE CENTER'S EDUCATION PROGRAM functions as an imaginative and rigorously applied response to the congressional mandate. The first national outreach program was the American College Theater Festival, begun in 1969 on the Mall under a tent furnished by the Smithsonian. The Center was thus an encouraging presence two years before it opened. By 1989, the festival had showcased more than 800 productions from about 600 of the nation's colleges and universities. After state and regional competitions, seven winners are presented at the Eisenhower Theater.

The Alliance for Arts Education (AAE), a joint project of the Center and the U.S. Department of Education, is a coast-to-coast partnership of artists, teachers, and school administrators committed to incorporating the arts into every child's education. This program owes much to the energy and early support of trustee Sidney P. Marland, commissioner of education and assistant secretary of HEW under Secretary Elliot Richardson. Marland was the first official to take a leadership role in the fulfillment of Congress's education mandate.

The education program came about when I introduced Marland to Allie Marriott, an active trustee and a strong advocate of the Center's public mission. We met over tea one afternoon in her home, and when Marland left he had been persuaded to set up an arts education program at HEW in direct association with the Center. He put Dr. Harold "Bud" Auberg in charge, and shortly thereafter Jean Kennedy Smith was recruited. Her leadership and imagination proved invaluable; largely because of her efforts and those of her brother, who was then chairman of the Senate Education Committee, the program has been the beneficiary of more than $2 million in annual appropriations. Lorna Clayton, former Rep. Orval

Hansen (R-Idaho), and Frances H. Breathitt have worked tirelessly as chairpersons for the education program. Tremendous credit is also due Jack Kukuk for the creative job he has done as executive director.

A third component of the education program (the college festivals and the AAE being the first two in terms of longevity) is devoted to children and youth. Introduced in 1976, a series of special performances held each fall and spring had by 1988 attracted more than a half million young people and their families. For the spring series, known as "Imagination Celebration," new works in theater or dance are frequently commissioned or presented. One year saw an updated version of Pinocchio performed by the Philadelphia Theatre Caravan in which the boy/marionette learns the traditional lessons of self-control and responsibility after being bombarded by video games and graffiti. Outstanding professionals and gifted amateurs—for example, Theatreworks USA of New York City, the Suzuki Academy of the Performing Arts of Mt. Prospect, Ill., and members of the National Symphony Orchestra—are brought to the Center for the month-long festival. The festival is then recreated at various sites around the country with the help of state AAE committees. Goals of the celebration are to support arts education programs in the schools; to provide a variety of quality performances on a regular basis to school groups and general audiences (one popular program, "The Symphony and the Sorcerer," effectively introduces children to the classics by combining magic with the music of Beethoven, Bizet, Grieg, and Tchaikovsky); to hold instructive conferences, workshops, and symposia for teachers; and to serve as a national model for replication by other arts education centers. In 1988 alone it brought 200 artists to 60,000 patrons.

With Very Special Arts, the Center has taken a pioneering lead in the use of the arts to bring disabled persons into society's mainstream. Founded in 1974 by Jean Kennedy Smith, VSA is directed by a national committee that sponsors an annual festival at the Center and conducts sustained outreach programs in all 50 states, the District of Columbia, and Puerto Rico. Its programs reach more than a million people in the United States and around the world. Marking VSA's 15th anniversary, a week-long festival in 1989 brought to Washington more than a thousand participants with physical and mental challenges, each prepared to demonstrate an accomplishment in music, dance, drama, creative writing, and the visual arts. Children, young people, and adults, they came from communities all over the United States and from 50 other countries.

Ever mindful that the performing arts convey a tacit statement about the national character, the Center celebrates America's rich ethnic heritage each year with the Cultural Diversity Festival. An outgrowth of the Black History Month festivals begun in 1978, the event now features artists of all backgrounds, and the music is likely to range from jazz to gospel to funk. Festival performers have included a Chinese storyteller; students from Washington's Duke Ellington School for the Performing Arts; and singers, musicians, and dancers from the Caribbean, Spain, Korea, Africa, and the Middle East. Although the festival invites performers from all over the world, it gives special emphasis to those in the Washington area, serving to fulfill the special commitment that Center trustees have to the local community. Like all programming of the Education Department, productions of the Cultural Diversity Festival are scheduled for both school and public performances. All school performances are free. Archie L. Buffkins has been responsible for many years for ensuring that the Center serves a culturally diverse community, not only in its performances but also in its operations and employment practices.

The 1989 operating budget for the Center and the National Symphony Orchestra was $54 million, about 4 percent of which came from the U.S. Department of Education, the Commission of Fine Arts, and intermittent grants from the National Endowment for the Arts. Almost all the money to run the theaters comes from ticket sales and private contributions. A major source has been the Corporate Fund, "a voluntary group of American business leaders committed to the support of the Kennedy Center as a national cultural treasure." The fund has a yearly goal of $3.5 million. The Center also relies on support from private foundations, as well as from millions of individuals of all descriptions—schoolchildren, college students, retirees, philanthropists, government employees, military personnel. Over a period of seven years, the President's Advisory Committee on the Arts has raised more than $3 million.

Since 1965 we have benefited enormously from the Friends of the Kennedy Center. Created by the trustees as a committee of the board, this organization has a Washington cadre of 600 volunteers who conduct free tours for more than 200,000 people a year, staff the gift shops and information desk, and assist visitors with disabilities. Each year they contribute more than 60,000 hours, equivalent to a quarter of a million dollars in wages. Mrs. Clayton Fritchey was its first chairman and served until 1969, when she was succeeded by the vice chairman, Lily Polk Guest. Both served with distinction, dedication, and devotion. In the early years the National Council of the Friends included trustees Mrs. George Garrett, Mrs. Albert Lasker, and Mrs. Jouett Shouse. The leadership continued with such persons as Annette Strauss (later to become the mayor of Dallas), Michael X. Morrell, and the very capable and energetic executive director, Thomas J. Mader (recently succeeded by Peg Allen).

The Friends early set as their purpose the development of programs that would project interests of the Center nationwide. It succeeds today through a membership of more than 35,000 from every state in the Union. One of its most publicized activities took place during construction. This was the Tom Sawyer project, which invited young people to paint the wooden fence surrounding the construction site. The fence was made up of 250 panels, each eight feet by eight feet. After 17 of them were painted by children in Washington's Widening Horizons Program, Sen. Leverett Saltonstall expanded the idea. Under his sponsorship, the remaining panels were painted by youths from all 50 states.

Once the Center opened, the Friends organized special tours as well as benefit events. In June 1985 they held their first annual open house, "Inside Out," a day-long festival with a variety of free family-style entertainment. It was part of the organization's programmatic obligation to make the national cultural center available to everyone, a point it makes implicitly and often in its publication, *Kennedy Center News*.

A much appreciated expression of this same obligation is the Specially Priced Ticket Program administered by the Friends, through which students, senior citizens, persons with permanent disabilities, enlisted military personnel Grades E1-E4, and others with limited income may attend performances at half price. During the fiscal year ending October 2, 1988, 70,000 tickets (valued at about a million dollars at full box office prices) were sold. The Center also offers numerous free entertainments, especially during the Christmas season.

Rarely seen by the public but regularly frequented by scholars and arts professionals is the Performing Arts Library, located on the top level and designed by the same architects, Philip Johnson and John Burgee, who did the adjacent Terrace Theater. The Library was created in 1976 as a joint undertaking of the Center and the Library of Congress. Through it, access is provided by video computer to the nation's most comprehensive collection of *everything* pertaining to the performing arts, including books, photographs, prints, music, recordings, and memorabilia. The library owes its existence largely to Daniel J. Boorstin, then librarian of Congress, and it was he who recommended Peter Fay to be its director. Fay had been associated with the music division at the Library of Congress, and there could have been no better choice. In 1988 about 17,500 people visited and used this library.

Activities of the Center go far beyond its walls. Undoubtedly the most shining example is the Kennedy Center Honors—in the words of the *New York Times*, "the closest thing that the United States has to federal recognition in the arts." This annual televised tribute has won both Emmy and Peabody awards. It once moved the *Christian Science Monitor* to call it "the American cultural equivalent of being knighted."

The Kennedy Center Honors were created by the trustees in 1978 to recognize once a year those who have made significant contributions to American culture through the performing arts. Honorees are selected by a committee of 150 distinguished artists selected by the board. The Honors are not designated by category although achievements in dance, music, theater, opera, motion pictures, and television are considered. Over time, the selection process has yielded a fair balance among the various disciplines.

At the project's inception, with the support of President Jimmy Carter, the Honors Gala was associated with the White House, and successive presidents have made it a tradition. The evening before, the secretary of State hosts a dinner at which the Honors are presented to the recipients. Next day the honorees are the guests of the president and first lady at a White House reception. The gala itself follows at the Opera House. There, the careers of the honorees are reviewed with film clips, performances by contemporary stars of the scenes or numbers that made the honorees famous, and interviews with, or testimony by, their friends and associates. Underwritten by grants from Merrill Lynch Inc., the performance is taped for delayed broadcast over CBS as a holiday special, and in recent years it

THE KENNEDY CENTER HONORS

'*Now it's time for our honorees to take another bow. They have graced our stages; they have graced our lives; they have graced our history. And that's the way it is. And that's the way it will be and has been for all of our century."*

—Walter Cronkite

1978. Richard Rodgers, George Balanchine, Marian Anderson, Arthur Rubinstein, and Fred Astaire with President and Mrs. Carter at the White House.

1979. Henry Fonda, Martha Graham, Tennessee Williams, Ella Fitzgerald, and Aaron Copland with Mrs. Carter at the Opera House.

1980. Leonard Bernstein, Leontyne Price, Agnes deMille, James Cagney, and Lynn Fontanne with President and Mrs. Carter.

1981. Count Basie, Cary Grant, Helen Hayes, Jerome Robbins, and Rudolf Serkin with President and Mrs. Reagan at the White House.

1982. Gene Kelly, George Abbott, Benny Goodman, Eugene Ormandy, and Lillian Gish with President and Mrs. Reagan.

1983. Elia Kazan, Virgil Thompson, Frank Sinatra, James Stewart, and Katherine Dunham, flanked by George Stevens and Nick Vanoff, producers of the telecast. Roger Stevens in rear center.

1984. Gian Carlo Menotti, Arthur Miller, Lena Horne, Danny Kaye, and Isaac Stern with President and Mrs. Reagan.

1985. Merce Cunningham, Beverly Sills, Bob Hope, Alan Jay Lerner, Irene Dunne, and Frederick Loewe at Trustees Dinner at the Department of State.

1986. Lucille Ball, Ray Charles, Hume Cronyn, Jessica Tandy, Yehudi Menuhin, and Antony Tudor.

184

1987. Perry Como, Alwin Nikolais, Bette Davis, Nathan Milstein, and Sammy Davis, Jr.

1988. Alvin Ailey, George Burns, Roger L. Stevens, Alexander Schneider, and Myrna Loy with President and Mrs. Reagan.

1989. Mary Martin, Harry Belafonte, Claudette Colbert, Alexandra Danilova, and William Schuman.

has been sponsored exclusively by General Motors. From the first telecast in 1978 the Honors program has always been hosted by Walter Cronkite and produced by George Stevens and Nick Vanoff. In 1985, the program was seen via satellite in more than 20 countries.

From another perspective, the gala has been important to the Center as a fund raiser. Each can be counted on to net more than $1,200,000. The chairman, from 1984 until her death in 1988, was the onetime child star and later successful television producer, Bonita Granville—or, as she was identified on the credits, Mrs. Jack Wrather. "Bunny" Wrather was charming, talented, bright, imaginative, and dedicated. She joined us on the board of trustees in 1972. We miss her.

REMARKABLY, THE CENTER has become the cultural heartbeat of the nation in a span of less than 30 years. What has been achieved did not come easily. Stevens, of course, deserves much credit. For his role in the Center's history he has received deserved attention as one of the five 1988 honorees and as a recipient of the Medal of Freedom, presented by President Reagan that same year. His successor, Ralph P. Davidson, was appointed in July 1987, coming to us from a successful career at Time, Inc., where he served as publisher and later as chairman of the Executive Committee. One of his primary goals is to raise $100 million for a joint endowment fund for the Center and the National Symphony.

As the Center moves into a second generation of leadership, it is good to remember what a monumental effort it took to build it and get programming under way. Prior to 1958, there was much talk about the need for a suitable facility for the performing arts in Washington, and there had been several abortive attempts to build one. Starting with the administrations of Franklin Delano Roosevelt and Harry Truman, enabling legislation was periodically introduced in Congress. Not until the Eisenhower administration, however, did the dream begin to take shape.

In January 1955, in his second State of the Union message, President Eisenhower made a serious commitment:

> In the advancement of the various activities which will make
> our civilization endure and flourish, the federal government should
> do more to give official recognition to the importance of the arts and

Ralph Davidson succeeded Roger Stevens as chairman. He's shown here with his wife, Lou, actress Sarah Brightman, and Andrew Lloyd Webber, composer/producer of the smash hits Cats, Evita, *and* Phantom of the Opera.

other cultural activities. I shall recommend the establishment of a Federal Advisory Commission on the Arts within the Department of Health, Education, and Welfare to advise the federal government on ways to encourage artistic endeavor and appreciation. I shall also propose that awards of merit be established whereby we can honor our fellow citizens who make great contributions to the advancement of our civilization.

A century and a half earlier another president had prophesied that some day Washington would become a center of the arts as well as the seat of government. But John Adams was painfully aware of the political realities, and he knew that it would be a long time before an insecure new nation could be expected to give the arts high priority. In 1798, in an oft-quoted letter to his wife, Abigail, he wrote:

> I must study politics and war so that my sons may have liberty—liberty to study mathematics and philosophy, geography,

naval history, navigation, commerce, and agriculture; in order to give their children a right to study painting, poetry, music, architecture.

Dwight Eisenhower may or may not have read this particular letter. Plainly, however, he thought the time had come to acknowledge, through some concrete action of the federal government, that the nation had come of age, as Adams had said someday it would. His signature on the National Cultural Center Act is one of his most personal legacies to the nation.

But it took many hands, and the convergence of many historical forces, to make a reality of the John F. Kennedy Center for the Performing Arts. The Center is a creature of Congress, but it is no less the creature of the affluent 1950s and of business corporations, private foundations, individual donors, the arts community, overseas friends, volunteers, and patrons. From the beginning it has been bipartisan, nonpartisan, and apolitical.

Like the free, dynamic nation that produced it, the Center today stands for many things.

It is a fitting memorial to a president who believed that "the life of the arts, far from being an interruption, a distraction, in the life of a nation, is very close to the center of a nation's purpose."

It is also the fulfillment of an ancestral dream long deferred—a dream as old as George Washington, who instructed Pierre L'Enfant to plan the nation's capital as both a cultural and a civic center.

Performances at the Center serve the purpose that Congress intended: "to convey to other countries some of the basic concepts of the American way of life." With equal effectiveness, performances by international artists convey to American audiences insights into other ways of life.

The Center is a magnet, drawing to the capital the best productions and individual performers from communities of all sizes all over America. It is, as well, a creative impulse radiating out to these same communities.

At its essence the Center is what its bylaws say it was destined to be—"a monument to America's . . . realization that the conquest of material things cannot stand the test of time until they find fruition in the realm of the mind and soul."

Appendixes

Acknowledgments

The John F. Kennedy Center for the Performing Arts owes its existence to the imagination, dedication, hard work, and perseverance of many people. This book owes its existence to these same people, especially to those who were active during the genesis period, from 1958 until the opening on September 8, 1971, and in the several years thereafter when policies and programs were being developed to fulfill the mandate of President Eisenhower and Congress.

On the lists that follow I have made an earnest effort to remember and identify many of those—in addition to our presidents and their wives—who shared this adventure with me, particularly in its early years. My sincere thanks to them all—and to the hundreds more whose contributions remain unsung either because of their modesty or because of my regrettable oversight or lapse of memory.

EXECUTIVE BRANCH

White House Staff: Gov. Sherman Adams, Earle Chesney, Fred Dutton, Myer Feldman, Homer Grunther, Bryce Harlow, Stephen Hess, David Kendall, Larry O'Brien, Gen. Robert Schultz, Maj. Gen. Howard McC. Snyder, and Rosemary Woods.

Bureau of the Budget: Percival Brundage, Phillip "Sam" Hughes, Elmer B. Staats, and Maurice H. Stans.

Department of Health, Education, and Welfare: Harold "Bud" Auberg, Arthur S. Flemming (the Center's first chairman), Sidney Marland, Elliot Richardson, and Caspar Weinberger.

Department of Interior: Frederick Seaton, Sen. Ted Stevens, and Stewart Udall.

Department of Justice: Carla H. Hills, Nicholas deB. Katzenbach, Frances S. Nunn, William Ruckelshaus, and Edwin L. Weisl, Jr.

Department of State: Lucius D. Battle, Andrew H. Berding, and Charles A. Bevans.

U.S. Information Agency: George Allen, Arthur Larson, Leonard Marks, Edward R. Murrow, Theodore Streibert, Abbott Washburn, and Charles Z. Wick.

CONGRESS

Senate: Clinton P. Anderson, Howard H. Baker, J. Glenn Beall, Wallace Bennett, Alan H. Bible, Caleb Boggs, Robert Byrd, Clifford Case, Dennis Chavez, Frank Church, Joseph Clark, John Sherman Cooper, Carl Curtis, Everett McKinley Dirksen, Robert Dole, J. William Fulbright, Roman Hruska, Hubert Humphrey, Jacob Javits, Estes Kefauver, Edward M. Kennedy, Robert F. Kennedy, Trent Lott, Michael J. Mansfield, Edward Martin, James A. McClure, Patrick McNamara, Wayne Morse, Claiborne Pell, Charles H. Percy, Jennings Randolph, Abraham A. Ribicoff, Leverett Saltonstall, Milward Simpson, Robert Stafford, Strom Thurmond, John Warner, Lowell P. Weicker, Alexander Wiley, and Milton Young.

House of Representatives: Carl Albert, James G. Auchincloss, John A. Blatnick, Edward F. Boland, Frances Bolton, Charles A. Buckley, Clarence Cannon, Peter H. B. Frelinghuysen, Eligio de la Garza, Kenneth Gray, William Harsha, James Howard, Charles D. Howell, Ben Jensen, Robert

Stephen Klein, manager of the National Symphony, with Leonard Silverstein, NSO president 1980-1983, at Mstislav Rostropovich's 60th birthday celebration.

George London and
Julius Rudel.

Jones, Carroll O. Kearns, Michael Kirwan, Elliott Levitas, Clark MacGregor, George Mahon, Robert McClory, John W. McCormack, Joseph M. McDade, Bob Michel, Norman Minetta, James H. Morrison, Thomas P. ("Tip") O'Neill, Melvin Price, Sam Rayburn, Carroll Reece, Charlotte T. Reid, Ben Reifel, Teno Roncalio, Howard W. Smith, Frank Thompson, Jr., Keith Thomson, Charles Wilson, James C. Wright, Jr., Sidney R. Yates, and Clement Zablocki.

Congressional Assistants: Dottie Beame, Robert Becker, George Bloom, Meron Brachman, Julius Cahn, Clifford Enfield, Bailey Guard, John Jackson, Barry Myers, Richard Sullivan, Nancy Vitale, Beverly Vitarelli, and Eugene Wilhelm.

TRUSTEES

Richard Adler, Howard Ahmanson, Joe L. Allbritton, Robert O. Anderson, Robert C. Baker, Daniel W. Bell, K. LeMoyne Billings, Daniel J. Boorstin, Frances (Mrs. Edward T.) Breathitt, Ernest Breech, Ralph P. Davidson, Mrs. J. Clifford Folger, Hon. Abe Fortas, Ethel (Mrs. George A.) Garrett, Bonita Granville (Mrs. Jack Wrather), Orval Hansen, Hon. Melvin R. Laird, Mary (Mrs. Albert D.) Lasker, Sol M. Linowitz, Sidney P. Marland, Allie (Mrs. J. Willard) Marriott, Harry C. McPherson, Jr., George Meany, Dina Merrill, Arthur M. Schlesinger, Jr., Catherine Filene (Mrs. Jouett)

Austin Kiplinger, president of the National Symphony (1978 to 1980), with admirer. The inscription from Maestro Rostropovich reads: "To my dearest friend 'Kipchik' with all my appreciation."

Shouse, Jean Kennedy Smith, Roger L. Stevens (chairman from 1961-88), Annette (Mrs. Theodore H.) Strauss, Amb. L. Corrin Strong, Henry Strong, Philip M. Talbott, Jack Valenti, and Lew R. Wasserman.

KENNEDY CENTER STAFF AND CONSULTANTS

Present Administration: Peg Allen, Iris Bond, Archie L. Buffkins, Peter Fay, Lenny Granger, Marta Istomin, Jack W. Kukuk, Patty Pacquette Laing, Eunice Larson, Laura Longley (for her review and comments), Thomas Mader, Joan Marcus, Geraldine M. Otremba, Jillian Poole (our indefatigable fund raiser), Susan Shaffer, George Stevens, Nick Vanoff, and Charlotte Woolard (as Roger Stevens's right hand she covered all bases.)

Past Administration: Joseph Addabbo, Amb. William McCormick Blair, Jr., Martin Feinstein, Thomas Kendrick, Jarrold A. Kieffer, George London, Mrs. Starkey (Cord) Meyers, Jarvis Moody, Alex Morr, Judith O'Dea Morr, Philip J. Mullin, Maj. Helen Roy, Julius Rudel, Claire St. Jacques, Clytie "Pat" Salisbury, Ann Schmidt, Aaron Spaulding, Leo Sullivan, and Vicki Welch.

Consultants: Maj. Gen. Chester Victor Clifton, Jr., Prof. Herbert L. Denenberg, Paige Donhauser, Robert Goostree, Dr. Cyril Harris, August

Heckscher, Roy Mascolino, Donald Oenslager, Carolyn Peachey, Harold Petrowitz, Leonard Reamer, Dr. Carlton Sprague Smith, Oliver Smith, and Edward Durell Stone.

Friends of the Kennedy Center: Ceci Carusi, Ruthy Cohen, Charlotte Dodson, Mrs. Clayton Fritchey (the first chairman), Ina Ginsberg, Lilly Polk Guest (the second chairman), Michael X. Morrell (the current chairman), and Jane (Mrs. Llewellyn) Thompson.

Ridge Press, publishers of *Creative America,* the National Symphony Orchestra, an affiliate; and the American Film Institute, the Washington Opera Society and the Washington Performing Arts Society, associate organizations.

FEDERAL AGENCIES AND INSTRUMENTALITIES

District of Columbia Government: Tom Arris, Milo Christiansen, Charles Duke, Charles Duncan, Judge Milton Korman, Robert McLaughlin, Walter N. Tobriner, Mayor Walter T. Washington, and Gen. Alvin Welling.

Fine Arts Commission: Charles Atherton, J. Carter Brown, Jeff Carson, and David E. Finley.

General Accounting Office: Joseph Campbell, Frank Kelleher, John Moore, and Frank Weitzel.

General Services Administration: William Casselman, Franklin

Lily Guest (center), second chairman of Friends of the Kennedy Center, with Lillian Hellman and Marta Istomin.

Henry Strong, the Center's vice chairman, encourages telephone volunteers for a National Symphony Radiothon.

Floete, Robert Foster, John W. Fritz, Jr., Lawson Knott, Joe E. Moody, A.F. Sampson, William Schmidt, and Karel Yasko.

Greater Washington Board of Trade: Clarence Arata, Everett Boothby, William Calomiris, Edward Carr, Leon Chatelain, Elwood Davis, Leonard "Bud" Doggett (who, with William Calomiris, changed the image of the board with community activities to what it is today), Henry Loss, Sally Scott Marriotta, William Martin, E.K. Morris, Susan Pepper, Charles Phillips, John Pyles, Jr., William Press, Victor Schinnerer, Phillips Talbot, John Thompson, John Tydings, and Osby Weir.

National Capital Planning Commission: Harland Bartholomew, Charles Conrad, Bill Finley, Samuel Fraser, George Oberlander, Mrs. James Rowe, Jr., Daniel Shear, and Paul Thiery.

National Park Service: Nash Castro, Bill Clark, Russell Dickinson, Manus J. Fish, George B. Hartzog, Jr., Don Heilman, Cornelius W. Heine, T. Sutton Jett, Joseph Lawler, William Penn Mott, Jr., Bernie Myers, John Parson, Joe Rossisvale, Robert Stanton, Conrad L. Wirth, and Nancy Young.

Smithsonian Institution: Walter Boyne, James Bradley, Leonard Carmichael, Peter Powers, S. Dillon Ripley, and Dorothy Rosenberg.

For Their Valuable Assistance

Janet (Mrs. Hugh D.) Auchincloss, Jean Bankier, Betty Beale, George Beveridge, Andrew J. Biemiller, Barney Breeskin, Paul Callaway, Jay Carmody, Richard L. Coe, Sheldon Cohen, Walter Cronkite and CBS, James Dixon, Ymelda Dixon, Charles E. Eckles, Mrs. Benjamin C. Evans, Jr., William Bragg Ewald, Jr., Vera Glaser, Norman Glasgow, Phillip Graham,

Archbishop Philip Hannan, Rev. Gilbert V. Hartke, Carl Haverlin, Helen Hayes, Christian Heurich, Jr., Paul Hume, Frederick R. Kappel, Rudolph Kauffmann, Samuel Kauffmann, George Keenan, Austin Kiplinger, Jr., Elizabeth L. Klee, Alan M. Kriegsman, Judge Theodore Kupferman, Jean Battey Lewis, Irving Lowens, George E. Marek, Hazel Markel, Benjamin McKelway, Marie McNair, Newbold Noyes, Bryson Rash, Mrs. Eugene Rietzke, Nan Robinson, Marie Smith Schwartz, Christine (Mrs. Roger L.) Stevens, Alice (Mrs. L. Corrin) Strong, and Al Zack.

Source Material

Kennedy Center Annual Reports, Kennedy Center and General Counsel, publications of all Kennedy Center departments, and *Stagebill;* Records and staff of the House and Senate Public Works committees, House and Senate Appropriations committees and staffs, House and Senate Interior committees and staffs, House and Senate District of Columbia committees and staffs; District of Columbia; Capital Engineers and historian; Air and Space Museum; Commission of Fine Arts; Greater Washington Board of Trade; National Archives; National Capital Planning Commission; Smithsonian Institution and Office of General Counsel; U.S. Capitol Architects Office; U.S. Department of Transportation, including

Susan Eisenhower, president of the Eisenhower World Affairs Institute, with Soviet Ambassador to the United States Yuri Dubinin and former USIA Director Charles Wick.

John H. White, Jr.; USIA; Washington Gas Light; White House, including Clement Conger and Rex Scouten; periodicals and newspapers; Patricia Baughman; Roxanne Kohlman, People-to-People International; Richard Oakland, Sister Cities International; Karine Zbiegwiewicz

John E. Wickman, Dwight D. Eisenhower Library; Harry Middleton and Gary Yarrington, Lyndon B. Johnson Library; David Stanhope, Jimmy Carter Library; Allen Goodrich, John F. Kennedy Memorial Library; Dr. Frank H. Mackaman, Gerald Ford Library; Douglas Thurman and Mary Kloser, Office of Presidential Libraries of the National Archives; the Nixon Presidential Materials Project; the Reagan Presidential Materials Project; Legislative Services and other departments at the Library of Congress; Katherine Roy, Martin Luther King, Jr. Memorial Library; Tammy Adle, Stephanie E. Burkhalter, Maggie Fogel, and James Dunn..

Brendan Gill, author of *The John F. Kennedy Center for the Performing Arts;* Howard Gillette; James Good, Smithsonian Institution; Martin Gordon, Corps of Engineers; Prof. Roger Meersman (for his able essays on the Kennedy Center); Elizabeth Miller; and records of the Columbia Historical Society (including the 50th volume).

Guillermo Espinosa, OAS; Harold Boxer, Samuel Rosenbaum, and Harold Spivacke of the Inter-American Music Festival; Jan Herman, Naval Observatory; Melvin Payne, National Geographic; Richard Freuchterman,

Trustee Allie Marriott.

Lorrie Secrest, James Ogul, and Martin Manning, USIA; Royce Ward, Watergate; Bates Lowry, Del Ison, and Francis Callahan, Department of Highways.

WITH SPECIAL THANKS

To William W. Becker, whose legal skills and acumen cut through a maze of problems like a scalpel in the hands of a good surgeon. He started working on the Kennedy Center in summer 1963 before his Harvard Law Schools days, and with utmost reserve and modesty he has contributed advice and counsel in the writing of this book, for which I am most grateful.

To Donald Lee Becker, an artful grammarian, who has reviewed and made a great contribution to the publication of this book.

To Kathleen Pagley Sidoti, my right arm, whose wisdom, pragmatism, dedication, and patience made this book possible; she has my everlasting gratitude.

To Prof. William H. Becker (no relation) of the George Washington University, an astute and supportive editor who helped me prepare my manuscript for publication.

The John F. Kennedy Center for the Performing Arts

*Governing Structure**

Board of Trustees

HONORARY CHAIRMEN
Mrs. Ronald Reagan
Mrs. Jimmy Carter
Mrs. Gerald R. Ford
Mrs. Richard M. Nixon
Mrs. Lyndon B. Johnson
Mrs. Aristotle Onassis

OFFICERS

Ralph P. Davidson
Chairman

Sen. James A. McClure
Vice Chairman

Leonard L. Silverstein
Vice Chairman

Henry Strong
Vice Chairman

Jean Kennedy Smith
Secretary

Charlotte Woolard
Assistant Secretary

Timothy C. Coughlin
Treasurer

Henry Strong
Assistant Treasurer

Harry C. McPherson, Jr.
General Counsel

William Becker
Associate Counsel

* *As of September 1989.*

MEMBERS APPOINTED
BY THE PRESIDENT
OF THE UNITED STATES

Joe L. Allbritton
Philip F. Anschutz
Mrs. Bennett Archambault
Mrs. Howard H. Baker, Jr.
Mrs. William Cafritz
Ralph P. Davidson
June Oppen Degnan
Kenneth Duberstein
James H. Evans
Robert Fryer
Mrs. Joseph B. Gildenhorn
Mrs. William Lee Hanley, Jr.
Caroline Rose Hunt
Mrs. Earle Jorgensen
Donald M. Koll
Melvin R. Laird
Mrs. J. Willard Marriott
Dina Merrill
Joan Mondale
Gerald M. Rafshoon
Mrs. Abraham A. Ribicoff
Leonard L. Silverstein
Jean Kennedy Smith
Roger B. Smith
Dennis Stanfill
Roger L. Stevens
Mrs. Theodore H. Strauss
Henry Strong
Lew R. Wasserman
Charles Z. Wick

MEMBERS EX OFFICIO
DESIGNATED BY
ACT OF CONGRESS

Louis Sullivan
Secretary of Health and Human Services

Lauro F. Cavazos
Secretary of Education

Bruce Gelb
Director, United States Information Agency

Sen. Edward M. Kennedy

Sen. James A. McClure

Rep. Joseph M. McDade

Rep. Charles Wilson

Rep. Sidney R. Yates

Marion S. Barry
Mayor, District of Columbia

Robert McC. Adams
Secretary, Smithsonian Institution

James H. Billington
Librarian of Congress

J. Carter Brown
Chairman of the Commission of Fine Arts

James M Ridenour
Director, National Park Service

FOUNDING CHAIRMAN
Roger L. Stevens

HONORARY TRUSTEES
Ralph E. Becker
Mrs. J. Clifford Folger
J. William Fulbright
Mrs. Albert Lasker
Mrs. Jouett Shouse

The National Council, Friends of the Kennedy Center

Michael X. Morrell
Chairman

Alexandra Armstrong
Joy Dirksen Baker
Heidi Berry
Mabel H. Brandon
Joy Carter
William Cotter, Jr.
Ralph P. Davidson
Geoffrey Edwards
Caroline Rose Hunt
Janet Lee Jones
Russell Lindner
Abel Lopez
Thomas J. Mader
Dr. Floretta McKenzie
Dina Merrill
Lisa Jackson Ourisman
Jock Reynolds
Susan L. Rolnick
Carol Schwartz
Norma Davis Smith
Annette G. Strauss
Henry Strong
Riley Temple
David Barclay Waller
Togo D. West, Jr.

National Education Committee

Dr. Orval Hansen
Chairman

Josephine Bever
Carole Brandt
Marta Istomin
Barbara Buchhorn
Jack W. Kukuk
Majorie Lawson
Harold Oaks
Ralph P. Davidson
Joan Mondale
Geraldine Otremba
Judith Kase-Polisini
Jean Kennedy Smith
Theodore Strauss
Ernest Boyer

President's Advisory Committee on the Arts

Herbert L. Hutner
Chairman

Margaret Archambault
Robert Bain
Joy S. Burns
Charles A. Camalier
Clair Chambers
Margot Denny
Ophelia De Vore-Mitchell
Mollie Faison
William Fine
Richard A. Gallun
Beverly J. Gosnell
Carl Halvorson
Leota Hayes
David Higgins
Stephen Jernigan
Peggy Mallick

Alyne Massey
Julia McCabe
Virginia McCann
Millicent S. Monks
Julie Montgomery
Lindsay J. Morgenthaler
Lillian Nicolosi Nall
Jim S. Nelson
Jeannette Nichols
Betty Noe
Kay Orr
John Pappajohn
John Piercey
Millie Pogna
Gladys Prescott
Chesley Pruet
Ann Rydalch
Huch K. Schilling
William Siems
Harriett Slaybaugh
Eileen Slocum
Charles Spalding
Richard Taylor
Dr. Paul Tessier
James Thompson
Judith Thomspon
Diane Ushinski
Dorothy Vannerson
Joseph Vetrano
Judith Woods
Naomi Zeavin

Additional Notes, Chapter 2

CITIZENS FAVORING CENTER ON THE MALL
(page 20)

Ralph Black, Mrs. Morris Cafritz, Milo Christiansen, Mrs. Frank W. Coolidge, Oscar Cox, Ladislaus J. Esunas, Lillian Evani, Hy Faine, James G. Fulton, George A Garrett, Mrs. George B. Green, Rev. Gilbert V. Hartke, Patrick Hayes, Edwin Hughes, Marie A. Hurley, Mrs. McCall Henderson Imes, Frank R. Jellef, Sam Jack Kaufman, Germaine Kretek, Hon. Richard E. Lankford, Herbert P. Leeman, Perle Mesta, Gerson Nordlinger, Jr., Mrs. Ernest Eden Norris, Marjorie M. Post, Mrs. R. I. C. Proust, Robert Richman, Curt Schieffeler, and Rachel Frank Skutch, all of whom gave statements. Letters in support were received, and made part of the record, from Leon Barzin, Andrew J. Biemiller, Robert Woods Bliss, Annabel Morris Buchanan, Edward C. Cole, Mary Cardwell Dawson, Clarence Derwent, Robert W. Dowling, John B. Duncan, E. R. Finkenstaedt, Duane H. Haskell, Elizabeth Butler Howry, J. C. Hunsaker, Mrs. C. O. Johnson, Joseph E. Maddy, Dorothy D. Marsh, Emerson Myers, Adm. Neill Phillips, Samuel Spencer, John S. Thacker, Pierson Underwood, and Eleanor Hale Wilson. (After the National Cultural Center was signed, many of these individuals joined us as advocates for the Potomac River site.)

FIRST BOARD OF TRUSTEES, APPOINTED JANUARY 29, 1959
(page 33)

General Trustees: Floyd Akers, Washington, D.C.; Winthrop W. Aldrich, New York; Ralph E. Becker, Washington, D.C.; Daniel W. Bell, Washington, D.C.; John Nicholas Brown, Rhode Island; Ralph J. Bunche, New York; Dorothy Buffum Chandler, California; John Josiah Emery, Ohio; Ethel (Mrs. George A.) Garrett, Washington, D.C.; Henry Clay Hofheimer, Norfolk, Va.; Frank H. Ricketson, Colorado; Catherine Filene (Mrs. Jouett) Shouse, Washington, D.C.; L. Corrin Strong, Washington, D.C.; Philip M. Talbott, Washington, D.C.; and Robert H. Wood, Texas.

Ex Officio Trustees: Andrew H. Berding, assistant secretary of state for public affairs; Leonard Carmichael, secretary of the Smithsonian Institution; Lawrence G. Derthick, commissioner of the U.S. Office of Education; David E. Finley, chairman of the Commission of Fine Arts; Arthur S. Flemming, secretary, HEW; Henry Gichner, chairman of the D.C. Recreation Board; Robert E. McLaughlin, president of the Board of Commissioners of the District of Columbia; L. Quincy Mumford, librarian of Congress; Conrad L. Wirth, director of the NPS; J. William Fulbright, Joseph Clark (D-Pa.), and Leverett Saltonstall (R-Mass.), three members of the Senate appointed by the president of the Senate; and Carroll O. Kearns, Frank Thompson, Jr., and James C. Wright, Jr., three members of the House of Representatives appointed by the Speaker of the House.

MEMBERS, ADVISORY COMMITTEE ON THE ARTS, 1959
(page 33)

Reginald Allen of the Lincoln Center; Marian Anderson, singer; Col. Earl Henry Blaik, formerly of the U.S. Military Academy; John Brownlee, director of the Manhattan School of Music; Paul Callaway, organist and choirmaster of the Washington Cathedral; Katharine Cornell, actress; Paul Cunningham, president of the American Society of Composers, Authors and Publishers (ASCAP); Donald Kirk David, chairman of the Committee for Economic Development; Mrs. James H. Douglas, Jr.; Robert W. Dowling, chairman of the board, the American National Theatre and Academy (ANTA) (designated by the president as chairman of the Advisory Committee); Richard Eberhart, poet; Dr. Edward L. R. Elson, pastor of the National Presbyterian Church; Karl D. Ernst, music director of the San Francisco Unified School District; Richard E. Fuller, president of the Seattle Art Museum; Rabbi Norman Gerstenfeld, of the Washington Hebrew Congregation; Martha Graham of the Martha Graham School of Dance; Richard J. Gray, president of the Building and Construction Trades Department, AFL-CIO; H. Hamilton Hackney, Maryland civic leader; Daniel A. Harris, professor of singing, Oberlin College; Rev. Gilbert V. Hartke, head of the Drama Department at Catholic University; Helen Hayes, actress; Herman D. Kenin, president of the American Federation of Musicians; Warner Lawson, dean of the Howard University School of

Music; Stuart F. Louchheim, president of the Philadelphia Academy of Music; Marjorie Post May, noted philanthropist; Howard Mitchell, conductor of the National Symphony Orchestra; Robert Montgomery, actor and television executive; Earl V. Moore, dean of the University of Michigan School of Music; George L. Murphy, actor; Joseph Prendergast, executive director of the National Recreation Association; Richard Rodgers, composer and producer; the Very Reverend Francis B. Sayre, dean of the Washington Cathedral; David S. Smith, trustee of the Noble Foundation; and Fred Waring, conductor.

Associated Organizations Assisting the Board, 1959
(page 35)

Academy of American Poets, Mrs. Hugh Bullock, president; American Academy of Arts and Letters, Lewis Mumford, president; American Educational Theatre Association, Inc., Dr. A. S. Gillette, president; American National Theatre and Academy, Peggy Wood, president; American Symphony Orchestra League, Inc., John S. Edwards, president; Music Educators National Conference, Alex Zimmerman, president; National Catholic Theatre Conference, Sister Mary Immaculate Spires, executive secretary; National Federation of Music Clubs, Mrs. Clifton J. Muir, president; National Institute of Arts and Letters, Malcolm Cowley, president; National Music Council, Dr. Howard Hanson, president; National Recreation Association, James H. Evans, chairman of the board; Poetry Society of America, Gustav Davidson, executive secretary; and Theater Library Association, George Freedley, president.

Index

*In July 1965 the author
was given this money
clip as a memento of the
first campaign to raise
money from private
sources, qualifying the
Center for matching fed-
eral funds. The inscrip-
tion on the reverse side
reads: "To Ralph Becker
with deep gratitude and
appreciation for all your
great and successful
efforts for the Kennedy
Center. Mary Lasker,
LeMoyne Billings,
Roger Stevens."*

About the Author

For more than sixty years Ralph E. Becker has divided his time between the practice of law and a lively career in public service and political advocacy. In 1928 he founded the New York State Association of Young Republican Clubs; in 1989 he was named Man of the Years by the Greater Washington Board of Trade. In between (to cite but a few of his political and civic interests) he has been assistant counsel to the U.S. Senate Election and Privileges Committee (1951); a member of the National Republican Committee; a member of the NASA Advisory Council's Task Force for the Commercial Use of Space; a principal in Lady Bird Johnson's 1964-68 Beautification Program; a founding director and general counsel of Wolf Trap Foundation for the Performing Arts; and president of The Voice Foundation, a New York City medical research organization.

In 1958 he was chairman of the cultural development committee of the Greater Washington Board of Trade. In this role he was instrumental in passage of the enabling legislation that led ultimately to the John F. Kennedy Center for the Performing Arts. A founding trustee and since 1980 an honorary trustee, he was the Center's general counsel from 1958 to 1976, when President Ford named him ambassador to Honduras.

Born in New York City, Becker did his undergraduate studies at New York University and obtained his law degree from St. John's University Law School in 1928. For military service in World War II he holds five battle stars, the Bronze Star Medal, the Belgian Fouragere, the French Croix de Guerre with Palm, the Netherlands Resistance Medal, and the New York State Good Conduct Medal. For distinctive contributions to education, peace and international understanding, he has been honored with the James Smithson Society Benefactors Medal, the Antarctic Service Medal, the Organization of American States Award, and medals or special citations from Honduras, Brazil, Austria, France, Denmark, Sweden, and Japan.

He is counsel to and founding partner of Landfield, Becker & Green, a District of Columbia law firm.

"There is a connection, hard to explain logically but easy to feel, between achievement in public life and progress in the arts. The age of Pericles was also the age of Phidias. The age of Lorenzo de Medici was also the age of Leonardo da Vinci, the age of Elizabeth also the age of Shakespeare. And the frontier for which I campaign in public life can also be a new frontier for American art . . . . I look forward to an America which will not be afraid of grace and beauty."

Excerpt from quotations from President John Fitzgerald Kennedy carved into the Center's river facade.

Photo Credits

The Acting Company, back endpapers 12.

John Bowden, x.

Richard Braaten, 88, 110, 112, 113, 116, 118, 119, 133, 156, 165; front endpapers 12, 13; back, 5, 6, 10, 11.

Jack Buxbaum, 114, 157, 182, 185; front endpapers 3, 8, 10; back, 1.

CBS, 181.

Capitol Glogau, 108.

City News Bureau, 44, 66, 71, 198.

Bill Clark, iv-v, 133.

Fletcher Drake, 109, 116, 117, 164; front endpapers 7, 9.

Mary Anne Fackelman-Miner, 185.

Fairchild Aerial Surveys, 24 (courtesy, National Capital Planning Commission).

Vince Finnegan, 56, 57, 59, 193.

Bill Fitzpatrick, 183.

Rebecca Hammel, 159.

Anne B. Keiser, back endpapers 3 (courtesy, Choral Arts Society of Washington).

Jack Kightlinger, 184.

Andrew Lautman, 13 (courtesy, Ford's Theatre).

Joan Marcus, 115, 116, 192; front endpapers 2, 4.

Bob Marshall, front endpapers 1.

John McShain, 106, 107, 108, 109.

Cliff Moore, 115.

National Capital Planning Commission, 59.

National Park Service, 9 (courtesy, Eisenhower Library).

Pryor-Menz Attractions, 119.

Bob Serating, 3.

Pete Souza, 184.

Roy Stevens, 111.

Martha Swope, 117, front endpapers 11.

UPI, 42, 82.

Van Damn, back endpapers 7.

Voice of America, 2.

Washington Performing Arts Society, 110.

All other photographs, courtesy John F. Kennedy Center for the Performing Arts.

The publisher is especially indebted to Bill Clark, visual information specialist, National Park Service, for supplying prints or slides of many of the photographs that illustrate this volume.

Designed by Chuck Myers
Copy-edited by Jane Gold
Printed by Maple-Vail, York, Pa.

Set in 11½ pt. Veljovic and printed
on acid-free paper.

Key to endpaper photographs:

CH: Concert Hall   OH: Opera House   ET: Eisenhower Theater   T: Terrace Theater

1. *Every Boy Deserves Favour* (Rene Auberjonois and Eli Wallach), CH, August 29-31, 1978.
2. *First Monday in October* (Jane Alexander and Henry Fonda), ET, December 28, 1977-February 25, 1978.
3. The Norman Scribner Choir.
4. *Jumpers*, ET, February 18-April 13, 1974.
5. Conductor Julius Rudel at *Ariodante* rehearsal.
6. James McCracken as *Othello* (Washington Opera production), OH, March 26-28, 1976.
7. *Porgy and Bess* (Houston Grand Opera production), OH, July 13-31, 1977.
8. Colleen Dewhurst in *My Gene*, T, June 8-July 4, 1987.
9. The Kirov Ballet (*Chopiniana*), OH, July 24-August 6, 1989.
10. Margot Fonteyn (The Australian Ballet) in *The Merry Widow*, OH, June 8-20, 1976.
11. Mezzo-soprano Shirley Verrett in La Scala's production of *Macbeth*, OH, September 7-19, 1976.
12. Spencer Beckwith as Benedick and Allison Stair Neet as Beatrice in Acting Company production of *Much Ado About Nothing*. Founded in 1972 by John Houseman, the Acting Company is the official touring arm of the Kennedy Center.

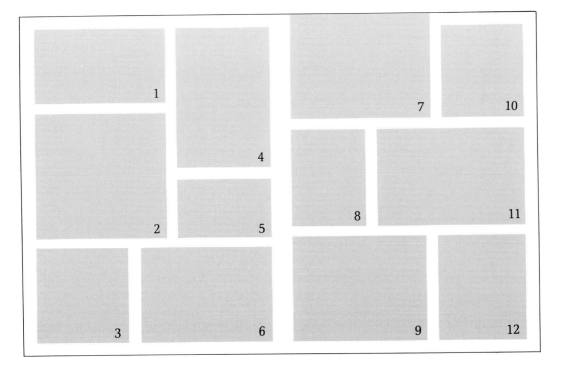